ENDORSEMENTS

"Who hasn't been worn down by the daily grind and wondered if there weren't a better way to live and lead? Who hasn't wondered if their boss really cared about *them,* rather than just how much they produced? In this heartwarming book, Joan Turley shares her journey to discovering how to bring out the best in the people you lead and to build a culture of trust that overflows with joy. If you've lost the joy in your work, let Joan inspire you to invigorate your joy and transform your workplace."

Jim Akers, author of *Tape Breakers—Maximize Your Impact with People You Love, Teams You Lead and Causes that Stir Your Heart*, Founder of ImpACTful Notes, and former Fortune 50 Vice President

"Work, eat, sleep, repeat. This seems to be our march to make a living, but the bigger question is, 'Are we truly living?' Our vocations can be a place of invigoration, growth, joy, and godly purpose. Let *Sacred Work in Secular Places* take you on a journey of discovery in your heart and workplace."

Gregg Matte, Senior Pastor of Houston's First Baptist Church and Author of *Unstoppable Gospel*

"*Sacred Work in Secular Places* reveals the divine purpose behind our discontent and despair regarding work. Simply put, we've been lied to. Work is not a curse; it's a blessing. Joan's writing not only provides a biblical, historical, and postmodern view of work, but also issues a clarion call to embrace our work as a means of partnering with God for the good of those in our sphere of influence. Work is our God-given platform, for the glory of God and for the transformation of cultures."

Paul R. Shockley, Ph.D., Professor of Bible and Theology at The College of Biblical Studies, and Co-Author of *Evangelical America: An Encyclopedia of Contemporary American Religious Culture*

"If you feel frustrated, confused, or stuck in your job, doing nothing about it will only make things worse. *Sacred Work in Secular Places* leads you to find purpose and clarity in your work and life, and why you should invite love into your heart. Every day, we have the opportunity to bless those around us. We have the opportunity to become difference-makers. Through her experiences, perspectives, and partnership with God, Joan's words will bless you, challenge you, and change the way you approach your work—as they have for me."

Joel Kessel, advisor, speaker and writer of communications and public relations; founder of Kessel Communications.

"If you're committed to making your life count for eternity, yet find the drudgery of the workplace stifling (or the darkness of the workplace overwhelming), stop everything and pick up this book! Joan Turley has penned her life message here, and it will change your view of work for good. Reading this book is like sitting with an old friend whose words of personal experience and biblical wisdom will carry you to a place of deeper spiritual purpose, no matter what your occupation."

Danny Rollins, Senior Pastor of Rolling Hills Baptist Church (Fairview, OH)

"Joan Turley's book *Sacred Work in Secular Places* provides a biblical and practical guide for the Christian seeking to find meaning in work. Whereas the world sees work as a nuisance, Joan rightly articulates that it is a calling designed by God, for His glory. I am thankful for her book, and I would encourage employers and employees alike to read it."

Joseph Parle, Ph.D., Academic Dean at The College of Biblical Studies

"One of the great discoveries made in the past few years is the sadly neglected reality of God's special care for those who do not have a calling for any specifically religious occupations. We have seen insight for the spheres, or mountains of influence, He affects. We can testify to 'marketplace ministries' that reveal His power to interact or intervene in the lives of many Christians with a concern for society who are involved in business ventures. Joan Turley's new release, *Sacred Work in Secular Places*, will prove another facet of findings into the question for God, 'What do you do on your day off?' that reveals that the rest of the week is actually His primary activity."

Winkie Pratney, Author of "Sacred Vacations—A Journey into Discovery" from *The Nature and Character of God Volume 2—As Revealed in His Creation*

SACRED WORK IN SECULAR PLACES

Sacred Work in Secular Places

*Finding Joy in The Workplace—
An Invitation to Partner with
God in a Beautiful, Broken World*

Joan Turley

AUTHOR ACADEMY elite

Printed in the United States of America

Published by Author Academy Elite
P.O. Box 43, Powell, OH 43035

www.AuthorAcademyElite.com

Paperback ISBN-13: 978-1-946114-18-1
Hardback ISBN-13: 978-1-946114-19-8
Library of Congress Control Number: 2016919286

DEDICATION

For my husband, Ken Turley: my best friend and the rock beneath my feet.

For the precious team of people who helped me learn to lead with love. You really were the sweetest part of those days, and I will love you forever and always.

For Jamie, Anita, and Francie. Thank you for making me a better person. The lessons I learned from the three of you launched me out of my comfort zone and into my Rehoboth.

DISCLAIMER

The stories in this book have been recreated from the best of my memory. Names have been changed to respect the privacy of individuals. I tell these stories with a grateful heart for all involved, but most of all for the lessons I learned from them.

CONTENTS

PART THREE:
WHY YOU CAN LOVE WORK:
BECOMING A DIFFERENCE-MAKER

PART FOUR:
WORK STRATEGY:
THERE WILL BE BATTLES,
BUT GOD WILL WIN

FOREWORD

I once posted a comment on a Facebook page about "haters" and a total stranger replied, "Well, you know, even Jesus had his Judas." That one, eight-word sentence piqued my curiosity and began a rich conversation that culminated in the book you now hold in your hands.

Turns out that Joan Turley knew a little something about haters and heartbreak. She had a story worth telling—and one definitely worth reading, too.

We live in a world where the job dissatisfaction rate has reached epidemic proportions. In fact, one recent poll estimates that as many as 80% of employees hate their jobs. This is not good news and something is terribly wrong. This alarming amount of unhappiness is seeping into the fabric of our lives and profoundly affecting our ability to experience joy.

Joan gets this! She spent years hating work. Caught in a vicious vortex of work-related depression, it just about cost her everything. Determined to break free and embrace a life worth living, Joan dug deep and hit the mother lode! She discovered the secret to finding joy in the workplace and now, nothing makes her happier than helping others find their joy too.

Get a box of Kleenex—even if you claim you're not a crier. Joan's stories of discovering joy in the workplace, to falling in love with the people she rubbed shoulders with, to learning to lead with love and impacting the lives of those she served, will leave you with water in your eyes and hope in your heart that your best working days are still ahead.

Read the book and rediscover the joy in the workplace.

Kary Oberbrunner
Author of *Elixir Project*, *Day Job to Dream Job*,
The Deeper Path, and *Your Secret Name*

ACKNOWLEDGEMENTS

Without these people, this book would never be. Ken Turley—You've always been the first to listen to my musings, my ponderings, my rants, and my ravings. You pushed me to put pen to paper and write what was in my heart—not to mention *publish* it! You, my darling, are the reason this book exists. Thank you for being this gal's best friend and lover. I don't know where I'd be without you.

Tamara and Nathan—With the exception of your father, you are the dearest loves of my heart. Thank you for letting me miss some important moments so I could see this book come to fruition. And Tay, that little man of yours—your little Joshua, my Grand Baby Boy—carried me through the long days of writing with his morning kisses and coffee-time snuggles.

Jan and Story— Before I knew my husband, children, and grandchild, you filled my heart with laughter and love. It was the three of us against the world! Jan, I am blessed to call you sister, and ever-grateful that you shared the love of your first-born child with me. Because of you, I learned to love more deeply and fiercely, long before our circle grew to include others. I love you both with all my heart! You will always be a part of me.

Nancy and Lynne—Where do I even begin? Sweet Mama Nancy, you have steadied my feet and kept me from falling more times than I care to admit. Whenever the devil whispered his darkest lies, you walked me back into the light of the Lord's unfailing love. And, Lynne, when I thought my heart was shattered beyond repair, you let me cry it out for as long as it took. Your friendship has always been a safe haven for me.

You are the best of friends, and I am a better person because of the two of you.

Gregg Matte, Senior Pastor of Houston's First Baptist Church—It was your sermon, "More Than A Paycheck," that brought my years of disappointments about work to an end. It gave me the joy of finally understanding that the Lord had chosen a specific platform for me. My work was a platform for God's glory, a place for me to love individuals whom He had entrusted into my care. I will be forever indebted to you for helping me discover that work was meant to be a blessing, not a curse! (And not only that, but that we who are called by His name were meant to be on-the-job difference-makers in this broken world.) I am so grateful for your leadership and your ministry. You have profoundly impacted my life and countless others'.

Laura Zeitner—I knew when we met that I wanted you to be my editor. I watched you pull out a bag of books you were giving away, and with every copy you held in your hands, your face lit up with joy, as though you were madly in love with every story. At that moment, I knew I wanted that girl to edit my book. And you have not disappointed. You have been an absolute blessing! I hope there will be many more stories for you and I to tell together.

To Kary Oberbrunner—Not only are you a best-selling author, you are the best coach ever! My heart is so deeply grateful for your willingness to help other people tell their God-given stories. I hadn't the slightest idea as to how to make this book possible until you. You—and your amazing Author Academy Elite and the Igniting Souls Tribe—have carried me over the finish line, and now I am an author! The words "thank you" are so utterly insufficient.

INTRODUCTION

SOMETIMES,
YOU NEED A NEW TATTOO

I t all started with that darn Thoreau quote. I was searching for God-knows-what on the Internet one day in 1999.
Without any warning, the words of Henry David Thoreau
popped up out of nowhere and plastered themselves across my
computer screen:

> *MOST MEN LEAD LIVES OF QUIET DESPERATION*
> *AND GO TO THE GRAVE*
> *WITH THE SONG STILL IN THEM.*

In the blink of an eye, those tragic words inked themselves
upon my soul. I was stuck in a job that sucked my confidence
and robbed me of my joy—Thoreau's words nailed me! All the
jobs I'd ever worked had labeled me Not Good Enough, Not
Smart Enough, Not Educated Enough, and on and on. Those
Not Enoughs took their toll on my sense of well-being and my
confidence, and dejection moved in like a houseguest overstaying
its welcome. Dang that Thoreau! His words sent me spiraling
into a tailspin of despair.

In the weeks and months that followed my crash collision
with Henry David Thoreau, all I could think about were pet

1

hamsters on their wheels, always running but never going anywhere. How in the world had I become like one of those stupid little rodents? I would get up, go to work, come home, pay the bills, pet the dog, kiss the kids, go to bed, and rise to do it all again, and to what end? It seemed there was nothing I could do to get off the wheel. Would I, too, go to the grave with the song still in me? Would I die unfulfilled with the ache of shattered dreams?

What was I supposed to do? I wasn't born with silver spoon in my mouth. My grandpa worked till the day he died—he dropped dead with his toothbrush still in his hand. At eighty-four, my sweet daddy was still a workingman the day he died. I just figured I'd follow their path, but I hadn't reckoned on the discontent. I hadn't reckoned on the deep depression. And I *certainly* hadn't reckoned on stumbling upon the words of Henry David Thoreau!

There was no turning back the hands of time. I had read his words, and I couldn't erase them from my mind. I knew that something had to give, or I'd never be joyful and whole again. So, I dove into the Scriptures and the writings of godly people who'd grappled with the subject of work. I was not disappointed! I hit the mother lode and discovered the redemptive intent of "Divine Discontent."[1]

Along with searching the Scriptures, I uncovered the writings of G.K. Chesterton and many other biblical scholars who had wrestled with the necessity of work and the discontentment that can go with it. Through this time of seeking and study, I realized that discontentment is a gift from God. Yep, you read that right! I discovered that discontentment is often a stirring-up by God, spurring us onward to what is yet to be instead of settling for what is. Chesterton called this a "Divine Discontent," which is God-orchestrated for specific times in our lives to remind us that this is not our home. Brief as our time may be, it is for a very specific purpose, and that purpose can be fulfilled through the work of our hands! That was my profound *aha* moment, and I understood for the first time that work was never meant to be a curse; it was meant to be a blessing. Work was meant to be our greatest platform for doing good.

Now that I knew the purpose for Divine Discontent, God's Holy Spirit planted a deep, abiding joy for my work within me. And, just like that, my perception of work began to change. The words of the old missionary C.T. Studd popped into my mind and plastered themselves right over Thoreau's words. This tattoo was bigger, bolder, and truer than true because it reflected God's call upon my life:

> *SOME PEOPLE WANT TO LIVE WITHIN*
> *THE SOUND OF A CHAPEL BELL,*
> *BUT I WANT TO RUN A RESCUE SHOP*
> *WITHIN A YARD OF HELL.*

How fitting that God should tattoo *these* words upon my mind, completely covering the lies of the enemy and proclaiming His truth!

I don't know what lies have been inked upon your soul. But this I *do* know: your life is precious, and you are deeply loved by God. Like me, you might just need a new tattoo. If you do, I hope you will grab a cup of coffee, sit a spell, and let me tell you a story . . . a story that just might change the rest of your life.

PART ONE

WHY I HATED WORK:
THE NOT ENOUGHS MUST DIE!

Somewhere around the age of five, I became deeply aware of God's love for me and of my need for His saving grace. So, I asked Him to be my Savior, and I put my heart in His hands. Through all the days of childhood, God was with me. Then, as I entered into my high school days, the nation experienced a move of God now known as the Jesus Movement. During that season of intense hunger for God, I discovered *God's Smuggler* by Brother Andrew. It was about a man who risked everything to get Bibles into the hands of people who lived behind the Iron Curtain, under a regime that persecuted Christians and banned God's Holy Word.

I had never read anything like that book. It completely captivated my heart. With the turning of every page, my desire to know God the way Brother Andrew did became a burning passion. Until then, I did not know that God could be experienced in such a deeply personal way.

The stories in that book lit a fire within my soul that directed the course of my life. From that moment on, the desire to know and serve God gripped my heart. I wanted to experience Him in profound depths, and God was faithful to fan the flame of that passion within my heart.

I thought the only way to serve God was to go into full-time ministry. So, when my life took an unexpected turn and I had to enter the secular workforce, I lost my sense of purpose. It was miserable. I spent years hating work and fighting depression. The workplace stole my joy and robbed me of my confidence. I honestly thought I had nothing of value to offer to anyone. Yet, somewhere along the way, I had embraced a few lies. I needed to confront those lies and break free.

According to the most recent Gallup polls, there is high probability that you have suffered in the workplace. My story could be your story. "The latest research reveals that 51% of people are not engaged in their work and an additional 17% are actively disengaged."[2] Discouragement in the workplace has reached monumental proportions, but there is a way forward—a way to love your work so much that even on your deathbed, "you'd find yourself wishing for one more day at the office."[3]

It's time to overcome life's roadblocks and rediscover the joy of work. In the pages ahead, I offer my story so that you might know *you are not alone* in the struggle to rise above workplace depression. In fact, God has a plan to restore love in the workforce—*you*! So please read on, dear heart, and may you find the courage to demolish every roadblock that has kept you from falling in love with the work of your hands. In the process, may you discover the blessing of "meaningful work, done in meaningful ways"[4] . . . with people you love.

CHAPTER ONE

OVERCOMING NOT ENOUGH EDUCATION

"All of a sudden I felt really tired, like the world had drained me for everything that I had."

Unknown

Once upon a time, I was an 18-year-old, green-eyed, blue-jean-wearing, long-blonde-hair-blowing-in-the-wind Jesus Freak who was gonna change the world. After I graduated high school in 1975, I headed to California with only my suitcase and a pocket full of dreams. "It's just a 3-month Bible course; I'll be back!" I told my folks. I would be attending a Bible training institute, and I just knew that my best days were yet to come. I was full of joy and as confident as all get-out in God's love for me . . . but that was before I encountered legalism.

It was introduced very subtly. God's grace and sovereignty were slowly pushed to the sidelines, and man's free will became the end-all-be-all. Where once I trusted God to carry me safely through the storms of life, now the responsibility of making it through rested squarely on my shoulders. My entire salvation depended upon making the right choice every single time. If I committed one sin and died before I had an opportunity to ask forgiveness, I'd go to hell. (At least, that's the impression I got from my teachers.)

Crazy as it may sound, I stayed for nearly twelve years. In spite of the legalism, I encountered beautiful teachings, made lifelong friends, and met my husband Ken. But before I found my way back to the grace and sovereignty of God, I completely lost sight of how very precious I was to Him. I lost sight of how very much He loved me. Legalism does that! It absolutely kills your spirit, crushing it beneath the weight of unattainable perfectionism. In all of history, there has only ever been one perfect man—the sinless Son of God—yet legalism demands that you, too, must be perfect, or you just might lose the favor of God.

Finally, my husband and I said, "No more." We handed in our resignations and limped our way back to Texas. It would be a slow healing for my broken soul. But God was faithful beyond words, and over the course of time He redeemed every broken aspect of my life.

Financially broke, spiritually battered, and with two kids in tow, my husband and I sold everything we owned just to make it back to Texas. We had invested more than a decade of our lives to a ministry that had toppled to the ground like the tower of Babel. How could we have missed the writing on the wall? We had given away the prime of our years to an organization we thought we'd serve forever. With its collapse, we were left with nothing to show for our life's work.

It would take years to rebuild the joy that cult-like legalism had stolen from me. Disappointment had led me down a rabbit hole, into a darkness so black that light ceased to even be a memory. Gone was my child-like faith, and happiness was a rare companion.

You see, more than anything in the world, I had wanted to be world-changer. Specifically, I wanted to be a supportive wife and a stay-at-home mom who raised her kids for the glory of God. I never wanted to join the ranks of the worker bees. My heart was in the home. Not once had I imagined a life in corporate America.

A RED SEA MOMENT

When we returned to Texas in 1987, the recession was raging, the oil industry was a bust, and unemployment was high. There were bills to pay and mouths to feed. My husband worked multiple jobs seven days a week just to put a meager roof over our heads, a little food on our table, and a few clothes on our backs. It was a pitiful existence. To be a stay-at-home mom was no longer an option. Begrudgingly, I took my place as a citizen of the working class.

I put on a brave front, but deep inside, my soul grew more bitter with every passing day. I questioned if God even knew where we lived. What had become of His faithfulness? To me, work was a four-letter word, and I hated it with a passion. This was not the life I had envisioned when I was that 18-year-old, blue-jean-wearing Jesus Freak. No! Back then, I was a daughter of the King, and anything was possible. At work, I was simply Joan Turley, insignificant and definitely *not enough*.

Even though I was disappointed in my life and often mad at God, He was incredibly faithful. One day I opened my pantry and there was nothing but bread in the cupboard! I looked over at my two hungry little children. Standing in front of that empty pantry, I shook my fist in air and said, "God, David said in the Psalms, 'I have never seen the righteous forsaken or his descendants begging bread' (Ps 37:25 NIV). Well, God, we've got bread, thank you very much! When you said, 'For I know the plans that I have for you, plans for welfare and not for calamity' (Jer 29:11 NASB), did you mean I'd *be* on welfare?" It was a terrible day, and I was not doing well with any of this.

No more than two or three hours later, there was a knock on my front door. When I opened it, there stood a woman I hadn't seen in several years. Her husband had been unemployed for a very long time, like mine, but he had recently found work. (My husband Ken had still not landed a job, at least not one that would provide for our needs.)

"Sheryl, I haven't seen you in forever!" I said. "What are you doing here?"

She looked me straight in the eyes, wagged her finger, and said, "God told me to come." She brought in bags, bags, and more bags of groceries: strawberries, peanut butter, cookies, vegetables, and fresh meat. It was an unbelievable, extravagant gesture of love from the Father. The children jumped up and down like it was Christmas morn, and as the tears streamed down my face, Sheryl handed me a hundred-dollar bill and walked out the door. All I could do was gather my little ones in my arms and tell them over and over again through my tears, "Never forget that it pays to serve Jesus."

In that beautiful moment God whispered,

Joan, you said that more than anything in the world, you wanted your children to know that the God of the Bible is alive and still does miracles today. In order for that to happen, you must let me take you to the Red Sea, for it is only in those Red Sea moments that miracles happen.

Years later, when my son was about to graduate high school, he reminded me of the story of the miracle groceries as proof of God's faithfulness to our family. He assured me that God would be with him as he made his way into a new life far away from our home. Though I had hated not having enough food in the cupboard, when I listened to my son recall that story of God's provision, I was beyond grateful that God had overlooked my bitterness and brought me to that Red Sea moment all those years ago—So my children might know there is a God in heaven who moves on our behalf.

And, oh, how I wish I could tell you that my disappointments with God ended on that day, but that would not be true. But, I *can* tell you that He never gave up on me.

DEFEATING NOT ENOUGH

Life in the workplace made me feel completely insignificant. It seemed like every day I spent on the job, someone labeled me Not Enough. If I'd heard it once, I'd heard it a thousand times in a thousand different ways:

> "You are not educated enough."
> "You are not smart enough."
> "You are not polished enough."
> "You are not corporate enough."
> *You are simply not enough.*

As I began to believe the lies that I was not enough, that girl who was once so full of hope slipped into the shadows for a very long time.

I had spent twelve years in full-time ministry, but didn't have a college degree. To hiring personnel, all that experience didn't amount to a hill of beans without a diploma to show for it. In their eyes, I was just an uneducated housewife. So, in 1991, I landed a job as a paraprofessional in a local school district.

Don't you just love that term, *para*professional? Every time I had to say the word, it was like an invisible little gremlin stood over my shoulder, reminding me that I was not a *real* professional. Not only that, I would never be one, because I was—you guessed it—not enough. I could only ever be a *para*professional. Ah, there it was again, that Not Enough label being pounded into my brain.

* * *

Most days, I felt lower than a dog licking the scraps under the table. Working within a school district meant being surrounded by educated teachers, who subtly reminded me that the opinions of the *un*educated need not be shared. It was, after all, an academic setting. I was not enough, and I never would be. The Not Enoughs were pretty much my constant companions. As much as I hated them, I didn't know how to cut them loose and kick them out of my house.

Fortunately, God was not finished with me. In the darkness of depression a light began to shine, a tiny light though it was! It would be many more years and several jobs later till all the Not Enoughs and Lies Believed were banished completely from my heart and home. Even now, sometimes, they knock at my door, but they're not welcome anymore.

Thank God for friends! I am convinced that I survived those bleakest of days because of the friendship of a faithful few. My precious friend Nancy constantly said to me,

"God doesn't care if you have a degree or not. He can place you wherever He wants to. He is not limited by your lack of a college degree—period, end of story! He is the King of this universe, and He can open doors for you that no man can shut."

Every time we met to share a cup of coffee, her message was the same. She spoke life over me, and she imparted hope into my despair. Her friendship was (and still is) a relentless reminder that God was for me, not against me, and that He loved me, warts and all. Having been steeped in legalism for years, I had forgotten how much God really loved me. Everyone needs a Nancy Briggs! The life-giving words she asserted began to break my chains, and that girl who had slipped into the shadows stepped into the light once more.

GOD AT WORK

The simple of act of remembering that God was faithful, even in the dark where I could not see His hand, caused a shift in my thinking and praying. I knew intuitively that somehow, someway, change was coming: kind of like the scene in Mary Poppins when Bert pauses mid-sentence, looks around, notices the wind is changing, and begins to sing,

Winds in the east, mist coming in, like somethin' is brewin' and 'bout to begin. Can't put me finger on what lies in store, but I fear what's to happen all happened before.[5]

Just like Bert knew that something marvelous was astir, I too knew that God was up to something. And, just as quick as Mary Poppins blew in from the east, God began to show up at my work in amazing little ways, proving to me that my lack of a degree did not matter to Him one *tiny* bit! I might have been a nobody to everyone else, but to God I was a somebody—I was His beloved child. He could and *would* move mountains on my behalf.

*   *   *

When I say I was a nobody, I mean I *really* was a nobody! During my time working for the school district, one of my jobs was to answer the phones. My day consisted of repeating the words, "Hello, thank you for calling XYZ Junior High. This is Joan, how may I help you?"

I was just the lady who answered phones, nothing more. I wasn't even in with the in-crowd of the paraprofessionals. When they went to lunch, I was not invited. I don't know why, but they never included me (and yes, it hurt).

I was at the bottom rung and had no clout with anyone . . . except for one school counselor, Laurie. She was well-respected by the higher-ups and deeply loved by the student body. She just loved people, and she loved me. More importantly, she saw the gifts that God had given to me when no one else did, and when the time was right, she drew attention to them.

One day all of the counselors were out of the building, attending a work-mandated training seminar, when both parents of one of our students were killed in a horrible accident. When the students learned this, a profound sadness swept across the school. As soon as the news reached Laurie, who was the lead counselor, she called the principal of the school and urged him, "Put somebody at the front desk to answer phones, and get Joan in that counseling office! For over a decade, she worked in a full-time ministry bringing hope to the brokenhearted. She is well-equipped to listen and extend compassion to our kids."

And, just like that, I was accompanied to the counseling office to comfort the students as they mourned that tragic event. In a building filled with highly-educated staff, God in His sovereignty chose to use an uneducated, degreeless paraprofessional to bring hope and healing.

TRUTH

A heart to serve, to pour into the lives of others, and to add value wherever you can will trump lack of education every time. A serving heart needs no credentials. It sees a need and says, "How can I help?" In the years ahead, I would be called upon to mediate disagreements between students and between teachers and to speak to the entire teaching staff on the value of mentoring. Although I was still an uneducated paraprofessional, in serving others and meeting their needs I began to experience that God was in the business of moving through people, *regardless* of their level of education.

Now, don't get me wrong, I love education. Both of my children have earned college degrees, and I am only a few courses short of an associate's degree. The lesson to be learned, though, is this: God is in the business of partnering with us right where we are. He is never limited by the Not Enoughs in our lives. All that He requires is a heart to serve people.

So, what about you? What Not Enough lies have you believed? God delights in you just as you are, and He is not limited by your Not Enoughs.

CHAPTER TWO
OVERCOMING NOT ENOUGH POLISH

"Hardship often prepares an ordinary person
for an extraordinary destiny."

C.S. Lewis

I overcame the roadblock of Not Enough Education and squelched the lie that I would never amount to anything more than a hill of beans. On the job, at school, I saw God begin to elevate the gifts and talents that He had put within me to bless others despite the lack of a college degree. Some days I even had a little swagger, pep in my step, and a big ol' smile as I walked the halls of academia! I had demolished a huge roadblock and thought I could tackle the world. I was ready for a new adventure—or so I thought.

A THING OR TWO ABOUT PRAYER

It was a Sunday morning, in November 1999, when everything changed. I was headed down the freeway with my family to church . . . and late, as usual. (I hate to be late. My husband?

Not so much.) Irritated and out of sorts, I popped a tape into the car's cassette player (Yes, cassette player—It was the 90's) to hear a message about the power of prayer. I thought rather smugly, "My kids and my husband had better listen up. They could stand to learn a thing or two about prayer!" I couldn't have been more wrong. *I* was the one who had a thing or two to learn about prayer!

The speaker of that message was a woman named Becky Tirabassi. She had been meeting with God in the early morning hours for over twenty years! Becky spoke about how to have a disciplined prayer life, but the exact words of the message don't matter. What matters is that it hit me upside the head like a two-by-four.

As I listened to the message, something shifted in the space between my two ears and in the vacuum of my heart. Suddenly, it was just me and God. And God said,

Listen up, it's time for you to learn to pray. Starting tomorrow, I want the first hour of your day. Put on the coffee, bring your Bible, and meet me in the morning.

I said, "What? You want me to pray for an *hour*? God, you know that every time I start to pray my mind goes in a million different directions. I can't even pray for fifteen minutes, and you're asking for an hour?" Under my breath and with gritted teeth, I continued, "God, don't you remember? I was in full time ministry, and I never learned to pray like I was supposed to. In fact, I failed miserably. I'm not one of *those* people, one of the spiritual giants who can pray for five hours without breaking a sweat. Are you sure about this?"

Yes, child, I'm quite sure.

The following day, an hour before dawn, I slid from beneath the warmth of the quilted covers and made my way to our cozy little kitchen. I poured myself a cup of hot coffee and sat down at the table. As I held the steaming mug between my fingers, savoring that first sip (there's nothing quite like that first sip of morning brew, is there?), I wrote out my requests. The first one was a dream that I had let go of years ago, back when the Not Enoughs first invaded my world. I wanted to write and speak. Don't ask me why I thought I could be a writer! Until that day, I had never written anything other than a few jumbled thoughts scribbled here and there. As for speaking, I had taught a few classes, but they were nothing to write home about. This was one of many hopes and dreams that I brought before God that morning.

Sitting at my kitchen table, dredging up old dreams and laying my heart bare before God was painful. There's an old saying, "Hope deferred makes the heart sick." Well, my heart had been sick for a long time, and it had become easier to stop dreaming than to keep hoping. Tragic, isn't it, that most of us give up so easily? Thankfully, God is relentless in His pursuit, and He never gives up on us or our dreams. Sitting at that kitchen table, I was completely unaware that God was fixin' to shake up my life.

A DIVINE DISCONTENT

For the next six months I got up early to meet with God. As strange as it may seem, my life did not grow more peaceful. If anything, I became more unsettled and deeply discontent. It was like craving the rich taste of a double espresso but being given watered-down coffee instead. The yearning didn't go away; it grew all the more insatiable. I craved the abundant life. I wanted a grand adventure with God—but, pardon the pun, I was stuck in the daily grind.

My life looked nothing like the stories I was reading from the Bible. I was working in a school copy room, running a copier for eight hours a day. Trust me, there was nothing grand or adventurous about that. There were days I thought I would grow deaf or die of boredom. The one bright spot of that job was becoming best friends with Lynne Fast. She proved to be the treasure of a lifetime. With the patience of Job, Lynne listened as I rattled on and on about my discontent and growing desire for something more. I couldn't have asked for a better sounding board through the emotional ups and downs of discovering God's purpose for my life. Lynne's friendship got me through a period of despondence that almost wiped me out. We're still friends today, and our families have shared a close bond for almost 20 years.

I still got up every morning to meet with God, but I was so discontent. I couldn't explain what was happening. The more time I spent with God, the more restless I became. My mind was bombarded with philosophical conundrums that left me with more questions than answers. Frantically, I searched for clarity, anything that would rid me of the discontent that consumed me.

*   *   *

In my hunt for answers I stumbled upon Thoreau's quote:

> *Most men lead lives of quiet desperation and*
> *go to the grave with the song still in them.*

I wished to God that I hadn't read those words—but I had, and I couldn't unread them. I felt exposed. Naked. Unmasked. I was one of those "men" in the quote—those trapped in lives of quiet desperation. I didn't know what to do to fix my life or rid myself of this unwelcome discontent. Why was I feeling this way? Had I missed my calling? Could I find it again?

It hadn't dawned on me that God was the pot-stirrer! He was the author of my Divine Discontent, the Holy Instigator behind it all. He was pushing me to wrestle with hard things, to delve deeply into the Word, and to find answers to those badgering questions that woke me up in the night and deprived me of my sleep.[6] Why was I here, and what was my purpose?

Until I could answer those questions, I could go no further. I was stuck and I was miserable.

I reminded God that this was not my plan. I never wanted to be a part of the workforce; I wanted to be in ministry. But I was stuck in a job I hated, and felt like I had missed His call, whatever that was.

Scared to death that I would remain in a state of quiet desperation, I read anything I could get my hands on about the reason for our existence and the purpose of our lives. Finally, in the summer of 2000, I stumbled upon Os Guinness' book, *The Call*. That book was like a gulp of fresh air for my oxygen-starved soul. My whole perspective on work shifted. For the first time ever, I considered that everyday ordinary work could be a calling . . . and possibly just as special to God as the preacher's work on Sunday.

Don't get me wrong, I still didn't want to make copies for the rest of my life, and I yearned for something more, but I began to wonder if work—more specifically, *my* work—could be what I was looking for. I wondered if there could be a greater purpose for work, one that surpassed earning an income. In the middle of wrestling with these ideas, I was unexpectedly offered a new job that would take me out of my comfort zone and face to face with another Not Enough, Not Enough Polish.

GOOSEBUMPS & CONFIRMATION

I reconnected with Elizabeth in June 2000, at the wedding of a mutual friend. Elizabeth was a former oil and gas executive who now owned a successful marketing and strategic communications firm. A week or so after the wedding, she called to offer me a job. I had prayed for months that God would open a door, *anything* that would take me out of that dreary copy room. However, given my new mindset about work, I agonized over the decision. If I was correct in my new way of thinking, then I had to have marching orders from God before I could accept the offer. The appeal of the job and the promised salary could no longer be the deciding factors. So, I prayed, "God, do you want me to take this job?"

At the time, I happened to be reading about the Apostle Paul, who worked alongside a married couple named Aquila and Priscilla. Like Paul, they were tentmakers, and the work of their hands supported their calling from God. I hadn't known that Paul was a tentmaker by trade. As I was thinking about Paul and his tent making, God interrupted my thoughts. It was as if He said,

Did you notice that Paul went to work with Aquila and Priscilla because they were tentmakers like him? Elizabeth is your fellow tentmaker. Her dreams, her passion, her creativity, are like yours. Take the job.

That was all I needed. In July of 2000, I turned in my notice and accepted Elizabeth's offer.

On the very first day of the new job Elizabeth drove me to her studio where the magic happened. On the way there, I shared the story of Paul, Aquila, and Priscilla—fellow tentmakers supporting their mission through the work of their hands. I said to her, "God told me you are my fellow tentmaker, and to take the job working with you."

Elizabeth grew quiet and said, "I have goose bumps. Just wait till we get back to the office and you will understand."

When we returned to the office and she placed a large blue file folder on my desk. Her eyes twinkled and she smiled from ear to ear as she said, "This is your first assignment, it's a corporate event for a great client. And guess what? It all takes place *under a tent!* It seems we are indeed fellow tentmakers!"

Talk about confirmation. That day, I knew unequivocally that God had called me to work there. Because the opportunity to work at the marketing firm had presented itself at a time that I was seriously seeking God, I thought the job would be all sunshine and roses. In reality, it was more like thorns and thistles.

(Just a note before we move on: It is a wonderful thing to have a calling from God. You don't *need* a calling in order for God to work through you, but wonderful things can happen if you have one! When you think you have a calling, though, I believe it is important to have confirmation. Confirmation has carried me through storms, and through seasons of wounding and deep testing.)[7]

NOT ENOUGH POLISH

My tent-making days began with great anticipation. Almost six months to the date from my first meeting with God in my cozy little kitchen where I had written down my dream to be a writer and a speaker, I found myself working directly for the president of a communications company, writing proposals and copy work for some of the biggest corporations in America. Only God can a take a little girl from a small town with no pedigree, college degree or fame, and with the snap of His fingers open up doors no man could ever open.

The joy I had experienced in the beginning dissipated in a matter of weeks as my boss critiqued my clothing, called my lipstick color into question, and rejected my jewelry. I was shocked. This was a battle for my heart, for the very essence of my womanhood. I liked my sense of fashion, but to my new boss everything about me screamed, "Not Enough Polish!" She had an elite clientele and an image to uphold, and I didn't fit the mold.

On one occasion, as we were ushered through the doors of a prestigious law firm to meet a prospective client, my boss pretty much told me to shut up and look pretty. I was to leave the talking to her and another, highly-educated, upper-crust employee, and no one would need to know I was a small-town girl with no education. This was just the tip of the iceberg.

Another time, I walked into the office with a new platinum blonde hair color I thought was *the bomb,* and she gave me that look of disapproval I had seen so many times. It wasn't long before she called me into her office and told me that my hair color didn't fit the company image. She handed me her credit card and said, "My stylist can fix that color. Here's my card. Tell him I sent you; he'll know what to do."

I was so mad that I gave that stylist a huge tip… on my *boss's* credit card! A few days later my boss stopped by my desk and asked, "Do you like your color?" I thought, *are you kidding me?* The dull, coppery color the stylist had given me was obviously horrible. I looked her dead in the eyes and said, "No." She replied, "Neither do I. He didn't get it right."

It went on and on. One day she would say, "What's with that dress? It has too much lace. You look like you're going to the Renaissance faire!" The next day I'd hear, "Are you really walking into that meeting with your hair styled like that? Tuck it behind your ears; it looks better that way." I could never get it right, and I began to second-guess everything I put on my body—from the color of hair, to earrings I wore, to the color on my lips and the polish on my fingers.

And then, one day, she said, "Joan, you may only wear clear nail polish, or a shade with the palest hint of color." Well, imagine my surprise when her favorite client, Katie Smith, waltzed into an event wearing *red* nail polish! (Okay, I admit, I secretly reveled in the fact that my boss wasn't on the up-and-up of corporate fashion trends.) I made a beeline for the nearest store and bought the brightest red polish I could find. The next morning, I sauntered into her office, fanned all 10 fingers in her face and said, "I'm wearing Katie Smith Red." Finally, I had polish.

Please don't get me wrong; I know Elizabeth meant well. This was her company and her image to uphold, but it was my identity that was being called into question on a regular basis. My self-confidence was quickly eroding. Almost every time I wrote a proposal for a project, I would be left behind when the time came to present it to the client. I felt like Cinderella, unable to go to the ball.

Time and time again, this scenario played out. Every now and then, I would march into Elizabeth's office and give her an ultimatum: If she kept taking my projects and giving them to someone else to present, then I was done. She would promise to never do it again, but I kept writing proposals and she kept assigning the presentations to other employees. I would cry and she would promise, but in the end, like Cinderella, I still didn't have enough polish to go to the ball.

Three years into the job, lots of heartache and lots of being left behind while others got the glory for the words I had written, my boss hired a charismatic new employee. I remember telling my husband, "That gal wants my job and she's gonna get it. I'm in her way." I was right, and it was only a matter of time before she worked her magic, strutted her stuff and elbowed her way into the boss's good graces . . . pushing me to the side. I reached a point where I had to choose: stay and be miserable, or walk away and pray for the restoration of my relationship with Elizabeth. I chose to walk away.

About a year later, in 2004, Elizabeth and I reconciled over a shared cup of coffee. The other employee had come and gone, and had broken Elizabeth's heart. I had a feeling that would happen. She cried, I cried, and together we mended the broken road between us. I'm so glad we did, because I owe so much to the woman who took a chance on me and offered me my job back when I was nothing but a girl making 5000 copies a day.

Knowing my future and all that was to come, God enrolled me in the school of hard knocks. You see, with Elizabeth's help, painful as it was, I learned things that would eventually make me a better boss to the hundreds of people who would be entrusted to my care. Nothing is ever wasted in the kingdom of God—even being criticized had a grand purpose. I learned that image did indeed have its place in the workforce. Because, shallow as it may be, man looks at the outside. Only God looks on the inside and truly loves us as we are, warts and all. In this world, first impressions are huge. It's like any new relationship: screw up the first date and you may never get the opportunity for a second one!

TRUTH

Want to know how I overcame the roadblock of Not Enough Polish? I embraced it! I let my walls down and took the criticism, hurt and all. And, by doing so, I didn't know it, but I was learning how not to deliver a message that would break another's spirit. I was being prepared to lead a dynamic group of people whose ability to perform at peak levels would depend on my ability to craft and deliver information that would garner buy-in rather than resistance. Once embraced, I was able to demolish the roadblock of Not Enough Polish.

Looking back, this roadblock was so very necessary. I began that job with not enough polish, and by the time I left I had plenty. Years later when God walked me into a job, located in the heart of "old money," I didn't bat an eye. I just donned my pearls and fit in perfectly! I had polish, thanks to Elizabeth!

Working with Elizabeth prepared me to take a team of Millennials and teach them that everyone needs a little polish. Creating great first impressions did not take away from their individuality; it only enhanced that which they brought to the table.

Have you encountered roadblocks that have absolutely broken your heart in two? Has a boss made you feel like you ought to keep your mouth closed because you don't deserve to have a seat at the table? Let me encourage you: you are precious and have much to offer. But maybe, like me, you need a little polish. Embrace your roadblock and let Him knock off a few rough edges. A little polishing may not always feel great, but in the end you'll be prepared for the door that God will open. Embrace it! You just might be a Queen Esther (Est 4:14 NLT) or a King David (Acts 13:22 NLT) in the making . . . for such a time as this!

Chapter Three

Overcoming Not Enough Leadership

"The Christian worker has to learn how to be
God's noble man or woman amid a crowd of ignoble things.
Never make this plea—If only I were somewhere else!
All God's men are ordinary men made extraordinary
by the matter He has given them."

Oswald Chambers

In July 2003, the job with Elizabeth came to an end. That charismatic new employee got her way. She made it unbearable and I had to walk away. You know it's time to leave when you pull into the parking lot and can do nothing but cry and wonder where you'll find the strength to face another day. I had no clue what would come next. But, I knew in my gut that leaving was the right thing to do, so I turned in my resignation and walked away . . . having embraced the roadblock of Not Enough Polish.

My next boss couldn't have cared less about polish. She had other lessons to teach me that would be equally valuable (and just as painful, too). I'm so thankful for these people who taught me so much, even when it broke my heart. Time, space, and distance helped me to see the real lessons I was being taught—lessons that walked me right into my sweet spot.

NO CORPORATE LEADERSHIP

After I resigned from my job, I used the extra time on my hands to volunteer at a newly-formed Christian nonprofit. Its fundraising goals would seem outrageous to any normal individual . . . unless, of course, they had met the organization's president and CEO. Katherine was a workhorse on steroids, and I mean that in the kindest of ways!

This woman was driven to make things happen for the people who landed on her doorstep, and she knew no boundaries. To this day, I have never met anyone like her. It was a great privilege to work with Katherine, but unfortunately, one that I did not fully appreciate. Pain has a way of blinding us and it is not until we can distance ourselves from the pain that we can see the lessons we learned from that season of our life. It was a painful season, yet I am convinced beyond a shadow of doubt that without it, I would never have walked into the sweetest days of my working life. I would never have discovered my God-given platform: mending hearts in a broken world through servant leadership.

In November 2004, only a few months after resigning from my job, my volunteer endeavor at the nonprofit transitioned into a full-time position. I was hired as the President's Executive Assistant and became the Director of Community Relations. If I thought working for Elizabeth had been difficult, I was in for the ride of my life. I should have been thrilled to be back in a ministry setting, but then I came face to face with another Not Enough!

Within the first few years, the organization garnered the attention of wealthy benefactors for its impressive work on behalf of those in need. As the organization received city- and state-wide recognition and awards, it was evident that additional staff members would be needed to fulfill the nonprofit's mission and vision. To borrow a line from Field of Dreams, "If you build it, they will come." Well, come they did! They were wonderful people who were talented, college-educated, and corporately trained in leadership. I, on the other hand, had none of these credentials. I had a decade of ministry experience, nine years as a paraprofessional, and three years of strategic communications, but no college degree and absolutely no corporate leadership experience.

It was a tough time. Among these remarkable staff members, I felt zero sense of worth or value. I am certain they had no idea how much I was suffering emotionally. It would have broken their hearts. They were really good people; I just didn't belong. I wasn't in their league. Though, it was ironic. As an organization, we lived and breathed to speak life into others, yet I was falling apart in the middle of it all. It took every ounce of courage to pretend things weren't so bad.

At one point, my coworker Hayden, who was less than half my age, unmarried and childless, implied that I didn't have the necessary leadership skills for my job. Come on! I thought. I had spent years in the ministry before this girl was even born, sold out to God at the height of the Jesus movement, given up my college years to be on mission with God, overcome a nervous breakdown at the age of 31, rallied my man to push through when he couldn't find work, landed my second job as a direct report to the president of a company, put both of my kids through college, begun attending college, and maintained a 4.0 GPA while taking care of a mother with Alzheimer's. No leadership skills? She was right, though: I had no corporate leadership skills. Hayden didn't mean to hurt me, but she didn't know how much pain I was in already. After her assessment of my abilities, I just shut down. I should have told her. But I was no longer treading water. I was drowning.

I value people more than projects. Always have, always will. But, the business side of the ministry was what kept it running. In order to change lives, they first had to raise funds. Fundraising wasn't my strength, and I could not flourish in that environment.

When performance reviews were mandated in 2005, I should have known it would be a losing battle. I had come to serve, to share my decade of ministry experience in support of the organization's mission, but instead I encountered another Not Enough—Not Enough Leadership. Frankly, this was something I never expected to face in a ministry setting. I asked Katherine, "Where in scripture did Jesus evaluate Peter, James and John's job performance? How can a labor of love be judged as unsatisfactory? Only God sees the gifts we offer to Him. He alone knows the value of what we lay at His feet and the purity of which our gift is offered."

We were down to the last quarter of the year and entering in to our hardest season. All of our energy was channeled towards one purpose, our annual fundraising gala. For several months, I worked seven days a week, sometimes more than 12 hours a day. To say I was exhausted would be an understatement. When the event was finally over, I hoped to kick back and celebrate all my hard work. Instead, I received a less-than-glowing performance review.

I was heartbroken, to say the least. How could I have worked so hard and sacrificed so much only to be presented with an unsatisfactory performance review? If my best was not good enough for the organization, then what did that say about me as a person? My leadership skills had been weighed on the scales and found wanting.

I'M NOT WHAT YOU NEED

The thought of spending the rest of my life running wildly on a performance-based hamster wheel was more than I could take. I dreaded going to work. Knowing I had missed the mark and would probably never measure up made me feel like a prisoner condemned to hard labor. I had nothing to look forward to, only incessant soul-robbing work. Like Much-Afraid in that classic tale of *Hinds' Feet on High Places*, loss of hope became my constant companion.

I remember crawling into bed, pulling the covers up over my head, and crying myself to sleep. The morning light brought no relief. The whole world felt gray, as if the sun had gone away. In the pale morning light grief just kept rolling in like a thick fog.

All I could do was cry, "God, help me." I choked out the words, "Will there ever be a place for me, a place where my gifts will flourish?" I wondered if I would ever be needed or have anything significant to offer to anyone.

I knew I needed to clear the air and talk to Katherine, but I just couldn't find the words. So, I borrowed some. With as much courage as I could muster and with tears streaming down my face, I walked into her office and sang her a line from a Dolly Parton song: *We both know I'm not what you need, but I will always love you.* It was an overwhelmingly bittersweet moment for both of us. In truth, we both knew it was time for my exit.

Looking back, God used Katherine to prepare me for sacred work in secular places. I don't profess to know the *whys* or the *hows* of God's intricate dealings within our lives, and I may never understand His timing. What I eventually came to understand and embrace is this: If our steps are indeed ordered by the Lord as His Word declares (Ps 37:23 ESV), then wherever our feet find themselves planted is the platform He has chosen for us to shine for His glory.

TRUTH

To walk with God means that nothing in your life is ever wasted. He will use every situation to prepare you for the platform of His choosing. So, in those moments of devastation, when your heart has been completely shattered by someone else's assessment of your work, give grace to one another, forgive those who wound you, and remember that your destiny is in the hands of God, it is never in the hands of man. God has prepared a platform for you—one of His own choosing—where your gifts and talents will shine for His glory.

Armed with the knowledge that God has a divine platform for your life, shall we take a look at God's ultimate purpose for the work of our hands? Read on, beloved, and you will discover that work was meant to be a blessing and not a curse. Whatever roadblocks you've encountered, kick them to the curb, send them back to the hell-hole from which they came, and go run your race. You were meant to shine for God's glory in the platform of His choosing.

PART TWO

WHY GOD LOVES WORK: A BIBLICAL, HISTORICAL, AND CONTEMPORARY VIEW OF "WORK"

B y this point, you know I spent years hating work. Now, it is my passion to help others find joy in their work and gain an eternal perspective of its purpose, one which far exceeds the monetary rewards of a paycheck.

Work, in its truest essence, is "God's invitation to partner with Him, through the work of our hands . . . in this beautiful but broken world."[8] Listen to me, there is a divine purpose for work. When we make that connection, we are on the road to discovering the sweetest days we will ever know this side of heaven. What God himself has revealed through the story of creation, that He is a worker, brings dignity to our work. Furthermore, if God, found joy in the work of His hands (Gen 1:31), is it not conceivable that as His image bearers, we too should find deep joy and meaning in our work?

Today, I am more convinced than ever that God intended work as a platform for doing good and bringing Him glory with the talents and abilities He gave us. Yet something has gone tragically wrong. Recent Gallup polls indicate that almost 70% of US workers are dissatisfied with their work,[9] and Deloitte's

Shift Index Survey states that 80% hate their jobs.[10] How can something God intended as a blessing be viewed as a curse? This ought not be.

When I gained a biblical perspective of work, it ceased to be a ball and chain and I found happiness on the job. I knew that my ordinary, secular work mattered. Moreover, as I began to see work as a partnership with God, work became infused with purpose and I walked straight into my Rehoboth: that place where God shines through the unique gifts and abilities He has placed within us.

Part Two is written to provide you with a biblical view of work, a rock beneath your feet for those weary days when you're tempted to forget just how precious your work is! It is my deepest hope that after reading this section, you will no longer view your work as a ball and chain, but as an invitation to partner with God in a beautiful broken world. Wherever your feet are planted may you be a light that shines brightly, a bringer of joy in the midst of the mundane, and a worker whose work brings glory to God and blessings to others.

CHAPTER FOUR

A BIBLICAL VIEW—WHAT DOES GOD THINK OF WORK?

"We live in a universe and in a history where God is working. Before anything else, work is an activity of God."

Eugene Peterson

Many books have been written on the subject of work. It is not my intention to compete with other authors who have written brilliantly and passionately. In fact, I champion their work. Far too many precious men and women have given in to their work-related depression and abandoned all hope of ever finding meaning in their work. I pray that a thousand voices be raised, pointing every weary and disengaged heart to rediscover God's perspective on work—that "work was to be sublime, joyous, and sacred."[11]

There is a joy to be found that can profoundly alter our mind's view of work: a shift so powerful that depression will no longer dominate our days or rob us of our true potential. We can love the work we do when we gain a correct understanding of its purpose. I know, work can be hard, and some days we don't want to get out of bed and face the world. Sometimes our bodies ache and our hearts are deeply wounded. I have lived those joy-sapping days, so I get it. But I'm here to tell you, there is a remedy for our sick and sore disengaged hearts.

I have been that disengaged employee! It cost me dearly. Consumed with the disillusionment of monotonous workdays, I disengaged, and not just from work. I disengaged from my personal life, too. In a state of work-related depression, I missed once-in-a-lifetime moments with family, friends, and co-workers. But now, I am no longer disengaged—because now, I know that God loves work! I mean, He *really* loves work, and if He loves it, then we can too. So, what do you say we take look at what the Bible says about work?

LIKE FATHER, LIKE SON

In his book *A Long Obedience in the Same Direction*, Eugene Peterson writes,

> "[T]he Bible begins with the announcement, 'In the beginning God created…'—not 'sat majestic in the heavens.' He created. He did something. He made something. He fashioned heaven and earth. The week of creation was a week of work. Right at the very beginning of the scriptures we are faced with the inescapable conclusion that God himself is a worker."[12]

Not only is God a worker, He is a worker who finds pleasure in the work of His hands. At the close of the first chapter in the book of Genesis, on the sixth and final day of creation, we find these words: "Then God looked over all he had made, and he saw that it was very good!" (Gen 1:31 NLT).

It's not difficult to conclude that, made in the image and likeness of God (Gen 1: 26-27), we too were made for work. We see this truth supported in Genesis 2:15, "The Lord God took the man and put him in the Garden of Eden to work it and keep it"(ESV). Like Father, like son! If God is a worker and He loves His work, His children should also be engaged in work and be able to find joy in it.

Many Bible scholars have concluded that because work was given to Adam prior to the fall, work was meant to be a blessing and not a curse. In the book *Our Souls At Work*, Dennis Bakke writes, "Sin entered the world and work got harder, but it is not cursed."[13] What a tragedy it would be for us to remain shackled to the idea that work should bind us! Once I recognized that God was a worker who was passionate about His work, and that His intent was that work should be a blessing for me too, I stopped seeing it as a ball and chain.

And then, one day, I stumbled on a quote attributed to Charles Ringma that captured what I truthfully believe to be God's intent for work. Ringma wrote, "Work is God's invitation to partner with Him that His kingly rule would be more fully established in this beautiful but broken world."[14] The very thought of partnering with God—*in this beautiful, broken world*—set my soul on fire. It was almost inconceivable—the very idea that God would extend His hand towards me, as an invitation to partner with Him—for the mending of hearts—in this crazy, beautiful, broken world eradicated every repulsive thought I'd ever had regarding work!

SECULAR, SACRED—NO DICHOTOMY

Earlier, I shared about a gem of a book by Os Guinness entitled *The Call.* In my opinion, he is one of the finest writers on the subject of calling because he so thoroughly defines what it is and what it is not.

Let me attempt to sum it up. (Please note, this is a very broad overview of calling, and doesn't do justice to the subject as so comprehensively presented by Os Guinness. My hope is that after reading my book, you will read *The Call* and become even better equipped to embrace your unique, God-given calling.) Guinness says that we are called by Someone (God), to Someone (God) and for Someone (God). This is our primary calling, and it is not to a vocation or location. The calling to something or somewhere is a secondary calling. These are callings, not *the* calling. Secondary callings matter only in relation to the primary calling. The personal, primary call from God is so strong that, once we accept it, everything else we do will flow out of our devotion to Him.[15]

As believers, we are individually called by God (primary) and then equipped for an eternal purpose (secondary) that is most often discovered through our work. Timothy Keller, author of *Every Good Endeavor*, writes, "It is through work that we come to understand our distinct abilities and gifts, a major component in our identities."[16]

When we respond to the primary calling, God equips us for secondary callings, then chooses our platform for His glory. While some people may have a calling to serve in a sacred setting, others may have a calling to serve in a secular environment. There is great need within both of these spheres, the sacred and the secular. Thus, whether employed in sacred work or secular work, if the work of our hands is in response to His summons, then all work is holy to the Lord.

The story of William Wilberforce brilliantly accentuates that there should be no dichotomy between sacred and secular work. (If you have never seen the movie *Amazing Grace*, the biographical story of Wilberforce's lifelong journey to end slavery in Great Britain, I highly recommend it.) For the believer, all work, be it secular or sacred, matters deeply to God. May you never be fooled into thinking that your ordinary secular work does not matter!

Guinness postulates that if Wilberforce had bought the lie that there was a conflict between secular work and sacred work, that one was better than the other, the abolition of slavery may never have been accomplished. Guinness shares that when Wilberforce first came to the saving knowledge of Jesus Christ,

> "his first reaction was to throw over politics for the ministry. He thought, as millions have thought before and since, that "spiritual" affairs are far more important than "secular" affairs. Fortunately, a minister—John Newton, the converted slave trader who wrote "Amazing Grace"—persuaded Wilberforce that God wanted him to stay in politics rather than enter the ministry. "It's hoped and believed," Newton wrote, "that the Lord has raised you up for the good of the nations." After much prayer and thought, Wilberforce concluded that Newton was right. God was calling him to champion the liberty of the oppressed—as a Parliamentarian.[17]

Having discovered his God-given platform, Wilberforce wrote in his journal, "My walk is a public one. My business is in the world; and I must mix in the assemblies of men, or quit the post which Providence seems to have assigned to me." Admittedly, you and I may never have such a large role to play in the course of human history. However, if we could "recover the reformational understanding of vocation: all of life, in every sphere and in every calling—lived to the glory of God and in obedience to his Word,"[18] it is highly probable that we would indeed see magnificent transformation in the lives of our coworkers and with effects that ripple into the lives of countless others.

In truth, "there is not a square inch in the whole of our domain of our human existences over which Christ, who is Sovereign over all, does not cry, 'this is Mine, this belongs to me!'"[19] Hence, our work belongs to God and is so much more than a paycheck. It is a vehicle for significantly impacting the lives of those who have been entrusted to our care and placed within our sphere of influence. Our work has a grand purpose.

In addition to having a grand purpose, our work is also for a lifetime. This is implied in Genesis 3:19 (NIV), "By the sweat of your brow you will eat your food *until you return to the ground*" (emphasis mine). In other words, God intends for all the days of our lives to be filled with deep, meaningful, purposeful work in wholehearted partnership with Him.

CREATED FOR GOOD WORKS

Knowing that God has called me by name and has invited me into a partnership with Him has had a profound impact upon my life: so much so, that it has kept me going even in my darkest days.

In 2009, I lost my twenty-two-month old nephew to tick-borne meningitis. It was a senseless and preventable death, which made it all the more horrendous. I have never experienced such intense sorrow and pain. The loss of a child is overwhelming. I loved that precious little boy with every ounce of my being. I was holding his mama's hand when she brought him into the world, I heard his first cry, and I cut his umbilical cord. It was love at first sight. To lose that child was devastating to our family. That little boy's death remains the most significant loss I have ever encountered . . . there is an ache in our hearts that will not go away.

When I returned to the solitude of my home after burying that precious child, I did not want to go back to work. I did not want to engage the world on any level. When we lost that boy, our world stopped while everyone else kept moving on. I know, life goes on, but it seemed so unfair. How could I be expected to walk into a place where people were laughing and smiling while my heart was breaking into a million pieces?

On the morning I was scheduled to go back to work, I sat with a cup of coffee in my hand and a Bible on my lap, covered in a cloak of sorrow. I can tell you I did not want to drag myself into the workplace. I did not want to talk to anyone, let alone see anyone's happy face. But in those early morning hours, before the crack of dawn, still and quiet, I began to sense God speaking:

Oh, Joan, don't you remember? I pre-ordained good works for your hands to do, and if you stay here wrapped in grief, you will miss the good things I have arranged for you. Work, my child, is blessing, not a curse. Don't sit out and miss all that I have designed for you—get up, my child, and go to work!

That little word of encouragement, "work is a blessing, not a curse," reminded me that there were blessings to be enjoyed— blessings that had been prepared for me in advance of this great sorrow. In the quietness of that moment, God reminded that He knew the weight of my sorrow.

He too had lost a Son, His One and Only. He also knew that in putting my hand to the plow, joy would come again. Ephesians 2:20 says, "For we are God's workmanship, created in Christ Jesus to do good works, *which God prepared in advance for us to do*" (NIV, emphasis mine).

As I pondered that God had prepared good work for me in advance of every heartbreak I would ever encounter, I remembered a message that my pastor, Gregg Matte, had once preached, called "More Than a Paycheck." His text was Colossians 3:22-24 and Thessalonians 4:12. That message was life-changing for me. It was the moment I finally understood once and for all, that my work, secular though it may be, was absolutely holy to God. And not only was it holy, it was a place hand-picked by God for me to shine for His glory. That day, I fell head over heels in love with the work of my hands, because I knew I was right where God wanted me.

I would love to share a little bit of Gregg's wisdom with you, with the hope that you too will know once and for all that your place of work is one of the greatest platforms you will ever have for impacting the lives of those who have been placed within your sphere of influence.

Let's begin with a review of the passages Gregg cited:

"Slaves [workers], obey your human masters [employers] in everything; don't work only while being watched, in order to please men, but work wholeheartedly, fearing the Lord. Whatever you do, *do it enthusiastically, as something done for the Lord* and not for men, knowing that you will receive the reward of an inheritance from the Lord—you serve the Lord Christ." Colossians 3: 22-24 (HCSB, emphasis mine)

". . . Work with your own hands . . . so *that your daily life may win respect of outsiders* and so that you will not be dependent on anybody." I Thessalonians 4:11-12 (NIV, emphasis mine)

As you look at each of these verses, can you not hear the underlying message? Work is for an impact, not just an income! Your job is the channel for impact. Gregg asked us to consider the following:

"Does it seem right that Jesus would die on a cross, Moses would wander through the desert, Paul would be martyred for the faith, Peter would be crucified upside down, and others would be slain with swords, so that today...you and I would acquire leather interiors? Does this seem odd? Or does it seem more right that all the above happened so that you and I could come into our work place *not just to have an income but to make an impact?*"[20]

Read it again, and again, until it resonates within your heart: we are in our workplaces *not just to have an income but to make an impact.*

TRUTH

God loves work! In listening to Gregg's teaching, I finally made the connection that God, who ordains our steps, sovereignly

places us in specific work surroundings. He chooses our platform and He places us where He needs a light that will shine
"in all of life, in every sphere—for the glory of God and in
obedience to his Word."[21]

Gregg challenged us to consider that whatever our title or
position may be, it's just a cover to usher in His love, that hearts
may be mended in a broken world. From that day forward I
saw myself as a Christian, disguised as a worker, with a mandate
from God to serve those beautiful people He had placed within
my sphere of influence.

The pages of Scripture consistently reveal there is no separation
between the sacred and the secular! His Word speaks not only
of priests, prophets, and apostles, but of shepherds, potters,
perfumers, bricklayers, educators, physicians, fishermen—the list
goes on and on—who were all called to live in faithful response
to God's call upon their lives.

Look at 1 Corinthians 7: 17. It says, "And don't be wishing
you were someplace else or with someone else. Where you are
right now is God's place for you. Live and obey and love and
believe right there…" (MSG) Timothy Keller says that in this
passage "Paul is not referring [. . .] to church ministries, but
to common social and economic tasks—'secular jobs,' we might
say—and naming them God's callings and assignments." He
continues, "the implication is clear: Just as God equips Christians
for building up the Body of Christ, so he equips all people with
talents and gifts for various kinds of work, for the purpose of
building up the human community."[22]

Oh, I hope you get it, and I hope it sets your heart on fire.
Your work matters; your light is *needed* in this dark world. So I
invite you to go even deeper with me, as we explore a historical
view of work.

CHAPTER FIVE
A HISTORICAL VIEW—
IS THERE ANYTHING
REDEEMING ABOUT WORK?

"Be who God meant you to be
and you will set the world on fire."

St. Catherine of Siena

N ow that I've given you a biblical framework for understanding that work is good and that "if God does it,
it must be all right,"[23] let's open up the history books
and take a look at the journeys of those who have gone before us.

I am not a theologian or a scholar, but I found immense
comfort in reading the stories of great men and women from long
ago. They had grappled with the very same things that threatened
to undo my world. Their thoughts brought me hope that life
and work could be filled with a sense of meaning and purpose!

THE EARLY CHURCH

Much of what I gleaned from historical accounts I owe to William Placher and his excellent book, *Callings: 20 Centuries of*

Christian Wisdom on Vocation. Beginning with the premise that "encountering ideas from the past can illuminate our reflection in the present,"[24] Placher's work gave me a bird's eye view of the journey we have taken: from the early church, to the writers of the Reformation, and into our postmodern world. With every societal change, our sense of calling and vocation has deepened and widened in response to those changes. Yet, despite an evolving interpretation of work and calling, Placher asserts, "amid all the controversies Christianity has preserved the fundamental idea that our lives count for something because God has a direction in mind for them." [25]

By shining a light on our predecessors, I hope to illustrate that our callings (the way we live out our vocation in response to His summons) becomes a vibrant portion of the legacy we leave to those who come behind. So, let's take a broad look at how calling and work have evolved over the years in response to societal changes.

For the early Christians (up until around 500 AD), figuring out God's call upon their lives meant deciding if they should even *be* a Christian—and if so, how should they live their lives in a world that rejected Christianity. Following their calling could cost them everything, from loss of family to martyrdom. Placher summarized the whole of this era as such:

> "What Christians had to decide was not what job to take but whether 'to be conformed to this world' (Rom 12:2), or to commit themselves to this community of 'aliens and exiles' (1 Pet 2:11) that followed Christ. That was the call—to respond to Christ's summons [His call] and then to decide how public you would go with it. For many this meant disinheritance from the family and for some it meant martyrdom."[26]

Those early Christians were courageous ones. They didn't have a buffet of choices in which to live out their faith; they had one choice: follow Christ and risk everything for Him. In bravely saying "yes" to Christ, they paved the way for the abundance of scenarios we now have in response to the call of God upon our lives. Bravo to those beloved and courageous saints of the early church!

THE MIDDLE AGES

After Christianity was legalized in the Roman Empire, it rapidly spread. By the Middle Ages it was the principal religion. Yet, even with the spread of Christianity, until the Middle Ages, most people still had little choice in anything—especially work-related. People did the work they were born into. If the papa was a noble, the son was a noble. If the mama was a peasant, the daughter was a peasant. In fact, "rising in society was a sign of pride; demotion was a shameful sin. Few opportunities arose for the child of a peasant to become a knight or a noble lady."[27]

With the establishment of monasteries, the opportunity to be educated and make something of one's life became a reality. For those who chose to enter the religious life, "a poor boy could end up a bishop, a peasant's daughter could become an abbess,"[28] and the issue was no longer whether or not to be a Christian but, "what kind of Christian should they be? The central choice for a Christian in the Middle Ages was—should I stay a part of my family, marrying, having children; or choose the priesthood or the 'religious' life in a convent or monastery or as a wandering Friar."[29]

An opportunity for education offered people the right to choose the life they wanted: a religious life or a traditional life. Until then, there was no choice, but the founding of monasteries and convents changed everything. Both men and women began to find their voices and impact their world for God's glory like never before.

The power of this societal change can be seen in the life of Catherine of Siena. Born in 1347, Catherine dedicated her life to Christ at an early age and gave herself to prayer, penance and works of charity (especially for the benefit of the sick). When she entered the Third Order of Saint Dominic at the age of 18 she became known for "mixing fearlessly with the world and speaking with candor"[30] to "people from every walk of life, including nobles and politicians, artists and ordinary people, consecrated men and women."[31]

Everywhere she went she encouraged people to ""Be who God meant you to be and you will set the world on fire." Talk like this had never been heard, especially from the mouth of a woman! Ah, such was the power of the option to choose religious life rather than accepting the station into which you were born.

But sadly, in differentiating between the religious life and the traditional life, the sacred/secular dichotomy was born. Some refer to this as the perfect life versus the permitted life. Os Guinness writes that during this time, "the perfect life was the life of contemplation reserved for monks, priests and nuns and the permitted life was the secular life reserved for soldiering, governing, farming, raising families. The permitted life… was a secondary grade of piety. The term *calling* was reserved for priests, monks, and nuns. Everyone else just had work."[32]

THE REFORMATION

It was into these times that Martin Luther burst on the scene and turned the world upside down, eventually germinating the seeds of the Reformation and recovering a biblical understanding of calling. Luther boldly proclaimed that the Scriptures did not support the contemplative life, the "perfect" life! To Luther, the contemplative life was hogwash, because the Scriptures declared that whatever a believer does in faith and for the glory of God is God's work.

* * *

Luther wrote,

> "The works of the monks and the priests, however holy and arduous they be, do not differ one whit in the sight of God from the works of the rustic laborer in the field or the woman going about her household tasks, but that all works are measured before God by faith alone...Indeed, the menial housework of a manservant or maidservant is often more acceptable to God than all the fastings and other works of a monk or priest, because the monk or priest lacks faith."[33]

With the reformational recovery of biblical calling, anyone could do God's work: from the peasants in the field, to noble lords and ladies, to monks, and priests, and nuns. All work was sacred when performed in response to the call of God. Luther's thoughts on biblical calling impacted countless theologians, who joined their voices with his. Together, they issued a clarion call for believers everywhere to recognize that work mattered greatly to God and was holy in His sight.

Joining Luther's position that all of work was holy, "William Tyndale wrote, if our desire is to please God, pouring water, washing dishes, cobbling shoes, and preaching the Word 'is all one.' William Perkins claimed "polishing shoes was a sanctified and holy act," and Bishop Thomas Becon wrote, "Our Saviour Christ was a carpenter. His apostles were fishermen. St. Paul a tentmaker."[34] All these theologians lifted their voices and proclaimed that work was a holy matter, a partnership with God.

TRUTH

God Loves Work! With every societal change, the Christian response to God's call upon our lives has deepened and broadened.

The early Christians had but one question to answer—Should I follow Him and risk everything? Their bold "yes" to God's summons in a tumultuous time paved the way for Christianity to spread like wildfire across the world. With the legalization of Christianity in the Roman Empire, the church flourished and founded monasteries and convents, which opened doors for ordinary men and women to have a greater impact upon their world. And while the "religious life" did create a sharp division between the sacred and the secular, it also created an environment for the Reformation to emerge, which led to the recovery of the biblical view of calling. The recovery of calling transitioned the world into the modern era, which brings us to me and you! How should we respond to God's call in a post-modern world? Turn the page, and let's take a look.

CHAPTER SIX

A CONTEMPORARY VIEW— WE NEED TO REDISCOVER WORK AS CALLING!

"God did not create us to live a reactionary life but to be co-creators in a meaningful life."

Victor Frankle

We have now examined work from a biblical view and through the lens of Church history. In order to see the impact of our work on today's world, we needed to establish that God is a worker and has called us to partner with him. It was equally important to learn that with every societal change, our sense of calling deepened and widened in response to those changes. Because, like it or not, we have entered into a postmodern world—a post-Christian world—where our sense of calling must once again evolve.

As we explore the significance of a Christian's work in this postmodern world, I pray that your work will distinguish you, bring honor to God, and impact the lives of those around you. Though we face challenging times, I am confident that our work profoundly matters . . . perhaps now more than ever.

WHAT THE HECK IS POSTMODERNISM?

If we truly want to partner with God through our work and impact the lives of our others, then we must understand the worldview of the people we work with. It is widely recognized that today's culture no longer holds the views once held in the modern world. We have embraced a new set of values. Therefore, if we are to impact our world, we need to adjust our approach to speak to a postmodern worldview.

In its most basic form, postmodernism is "characterized by a rejection of absolute truth."[35] All truth is now seen as relative: in other words, what is true for one person may not be true for another. (They are absolutely sure that there are no absolutes!) "Postmodernism, as a worldview, refuses to allow any single defining source for truth and reality. The new emphasis is on difference, plurality and selective forms of tolerance."[36]

A TIME FOR ACTION

That's where we are, folks. We're living in world that no longer believes in absolute truth. However, even though we live in a world where truth no longer matters and Christianity is seen as narrow and intolerant, we still have opportunities. Regardless of its worldview, every human heart remains the same—in need of healing and deep compassion. God has established work as a means of connection with those who need His grace and mercy. This is not the time to shrink back from seeming "too Christian." This is the time to live out the gospel!

I think this could be our finest hour. With truth being challenged and Christianity called into question, the postmodern era bears a striking resemblance to the days of the early church. Indeed, they were difficult days for Christians, yet because the love of God was so outstandingly demonstrated through the lives of the early saints, the message of God and His love for mankind flourished in that hostile world. Like the early saints, it is of utmost importance that our actions speak louder than our words.

In his book, *Every Good Endeavor*, Timothy Keller shares the story of a woman who made a big mistake at her new job—a mistake that could have gotten her fired. But instead, her boss went to his superior and took responsibility for her mistake. In doing so, he lost some of his reputation and good standing. The woman couldn't understand why her boss would take the blame for her! She kept asking him why, *why* would he do that for her? Finally, he relented and told her, "I am a Christian. That means among other things that God accepts me because Jesus Christ took the blame for things that I have done wrong. He did that on the cross. That is why I have the desire and sometimes the ability to take the blame for others."[37] In response, the woman simply asked him where he went to church! The Christ-like selflessness of her boss was a transformative force in this woman's life.

While it may not be as culturally acceptable to openly share the Gospel, nothing can prevent us from living it. When we allow the gospel to shape our character and our actions toward others, the world takes notice and is attracted to the Gospel.

We are given a huge opportunity to make a difference in the workplace when we choose to "respect and treat those who believe differently as valued equals in the workplace and at the same time . . . be unashamed to be identified with Jesus"[38]. In this postmodern world our actions matter: not just in how we treat our co-workers, but also in the quality of our work. "As we do good work that reflects God's character graciously, purely, morally, ethically, creatively, and excellently, we unleash His beauty. People see God."[39] Our work is the greatest platform we have to express God's desire to mend the wounded hearts of His beloved children. So do good work and get noticed—not for your sake, but that your circle of influence might grow for the blessing of many! We are called to serve that others might come to know the Love that has transformed our lives.

Here's the deal: your workplace is filled with people who are brokenhearted. Find a way to connect and show some love! I fell in love with work when I fell in love with the people, plain and simple. In today's postmodern world our workplaces are a wonderful melting pot of every culture and race. If we see our work as a place to love others, I promise you, beautiful things will happen. Just start looking for creative ways to show others they are of immeasurable worth, simply because they are made in the image of God.

I will never forget the time that a friend of mine at work, Adiva, shared with me that her sister was going through a painful divorce and was moving back to be near my friend and her extended family. Her sister was a precious single mom, raising two adorable little boys, and the three of them had endured great rejection and loss of love. It was a painful time for her sister and the whole family.

I asked Adiva if we could throw a housewarming party for her sister. She tilted her head and gave me a blank look. "What's a housewarming party?" she asked. You see, Adiva was from a completely different culture and religion and had never heard of the concept! I explained what it was, and that I believed if we could gather a group of women together for the purpose of loving and encouraging her sister's heart, it just might lighten her load just a bit. So, we did it! An unlikely, diverse group of Christian, Jewish, and Muslim women gathered in that room, and we laughed, cried, and prayed for a bright new future for Adiva's sister. *That* is how loving your neighbor as yourself is done!

TRUTH

God loves work! The memory of all those women's beautiful faces, gathered together to offer love and support for a fellow human being, brings such happiness to my heart. It's moments like those that make our work an absolute joy. In today's postmodern world, our work is relational. "God wants us to use our gifts and talents to make something wonderful happen. We are made in the image of God as individuals, but are put in families and companies to work. This is the essence of a joyful workplace. In this modern age, God likes to use people involved in business for the carrying out of the great commandment to love and serve our neighbors as ourselves."[40]

Oh, I hope you are beginning to see just how significant a platform our work is when it comes to impacting the lives of those with whom we work. Are you ready to discover why you, too, can absolutely *love* work the way God does? Turn the page and discover the joy of falling in love with work and becoming a difference-maker in a postmodern world.

PART THREE

WHY YOU CAN LOVE WORK: BECOMING A DIFFERENCE-MAKER

I n the time leading up to my departure from the Christian nonprofit, I felt deeply discouraged. But one day, I picked up my Bible and stumbled into a story that changed everything!

There was a man named Isaac who dug a well. After he finished, some neighboring herdsmen came and claimed it as their own. Rather than quarrel and stir up strife, Isaac moved on and dug another well. (*Been there, done that,* I thought. That reminded me of my experience with Elizabeth.) Again, more herdsmen came and claimed this well too. (Hmm, that reminded me of all the professionals at the nonprofit who quickly outshone me and made my work redundant. This story was hitting close to home.) So, Isaac moved on and built a third well. This time, no one came to steal the work of his hands! Isaac called the well Rehoboth, which means "room enough for me"(Gen 26:19-24 ESV). *Oh my gosh.* That was exactly what I been praying for—a place where there would be room enough for me.

That word, Rehoboth, became an anchor for my soul. I began to pray over and over, "God, if I must work, please bring me to that place where there is room enough for me. Bring me to a place where my gifts will shine for your glory. Would you bring me to Rehoboth?"

Within weeks of stumbling upon that story of Isaac and his wells, God intervened in the middle of my brokenness and led me to a place where there was finally room enough for me. As I was praying for Rehoboth, my boss, Katherine, was praying for me too. She prayed that God would bring me to a "safe place." In fact, she approached her friend, the CEO of a salon and spa, and asked if she had a position open for me. In February 2006, I was hired as Client Appointment Coordinator.

And oh, yes—the Not Enough Leadership roadblock was smashed to smithereens as I flourished in my Rehoboth. I walked into my destiny, the sweet spot God had been preparing for me all those years ago when I first met Him in the morning at my cozy kitchen table.

There is a Rehoboth for every child of God. I do not know how many wells you may have to dig, but don't quarrel when someone steals your well. Move on, dear child, and dig another, knowing that the next one you dig could be your Rehoboth.

This book has been written for all of you that desperately long for your own Rehoboth. Life is hard, and we never fully arrive this side of heaven; but we do get glimpses of His magnificent hand divinely placed upon our lives. As we share those moments in our lives with one another, when suddenly the clouds part and we see His plan . . . that is when we encourage one another to stay the course and rediscover that we, like the saints of old, have been called by a Most Holy God. I offer you my simple stories, stories of an ordinary working woman, who has discovered that Work is more than a paycheck; it's an amazing platform for His glory. It's a partnership with God.

CHAPTER SEVEN
BEING GRACE-GIVERS
AND LOVE-LEADERS

*"It is God's job to judge; it is the Holy Spirit's job to convict;
it is my job to love."*

Billy Graham

I must confess, I went to my new job kicking and scream-
ing. Had it not been for my husband, who gently told me,
"Give it a try; this just might be the best job you've ever
had," I'm not sure I would have walked through those doors.
Terrified of the unknown and unsure of my place in a nonreli-
gious setting, like Wilberforce, I almost missed my calling and
the sweetest working days I've ever known.

HE SENT ME TO BABYLON

As I opened the glass doors of the salon and walked through, I
nearly stopped in my tracks. I was definitely not in Kansas anymore! There were guys and gals; divas, straights and gays; blue
haired biddies, blonde haired bombshells, pink haired punks,
and everything in between. Gone was the nest-like safety of

the ministry environment I had just left. I was thrust into the world of glitz and glamour and the high-dollar pursuit of beauty at any cost. Under my breath I muttered, "Oh my Lord, you have sent me to Babylon." It was culture shock, to say the least!

As I transitioned from the "sacred" atmosphere of the nonprofit to this new secular setting, my world was rocked quite a bit. I had a lot of things to learn. The different environments between the nonprofit and the new job couldn't have been more extreme. The former culture was ultra conservative and black and white with room for little grey. Lord have mercy, the salon world was anything but conservative! It was a melting pot of colorful people with political and religious views that were often the polar opposite of mine. I had to learn how to love people—not just in word, but in deed—who did not share my personal beliefs.

Who would have thought I would find my calling in Babylon? Not me! Yet, it was in Babylon that I finally grasped the truth that there was no disparity between sacred and the secular. All work is holy when we choose to partner with God. In Babylon, I fell in love with the people He sent me to serve, and it was there that my work became more than a paycheck. In partnering with God (in Babylon of all places), ordinary days soon gave way to extraordinary, joy-filled ones as love became the driving force behind the work of my hands.

But first, I had to learn how to genuinely love and care for those who didn't share my convictions. More specifically, I had to learn that it was God's job to judge, not mine; and it was the Holy Spirit's job to convict, not mine. My job was to love, that's all, and the best way I could learn to love them was to serve them with my whole heart. It sounds simple, but it wasn't . . . not at all. God had to orchestrate some events that went against my grain, but ultimately taught me how to love even when everything within me wanted to slap the living daylights out of someone!

CHEWED UP AND SPIT OUT

I could see the anger on her face as she came charging towards the counter I stood behind. What in the world could have made Kim so mad? At that moment, I was really thankful for the counter between us, but no physical barrier could protect me from her verbal onslaught. She was loud, she was rude and obnoxious to say the least, and everybody within earshot knew that I was getting the full force of Kim's anger. Someone had made a mistake in booking Kim's appointments, and someone was going to pay for it.

Wave after wave, she ripped me to shreds in front of co-workers and clients. Warm tears rose in my eyes and I tried to blink them back. Everyone was looking at me. I stood there completely humiliated. In all my years in the workforce I had never seen such unprofessionalism. Never had I been the punching bag of a co-worker's tyrannical behavior. But then again, I had pretty much worked in safe places—this was Babylon, and these were her people. It was surreal; it seemed like everything moved in slow motion as I looked around to observe the shock on people's faces. She had made a fool of herself, but that didn't comfort me at all. How I found my voice, I will never know. With little more than I whisper I simply said, "Excuse me," walked away to a private corner, and fell apart.

Alone and feeling sorry for myself, I let the tears flow freely. As I tried to calm myself down and get a handle on what had just happen, I seemed to hear God say, Go serve Kim. I was outraged. I couldn't believe that God would actually ask me to go serve that woman who had just been so mean to me. I looked up at the ceiling as though I was staring into the face of God. "God, did you not see what just happened?" I said. "Didn't you see how she treated me? She just chewed me up and spit me out in front of everyone. I am not the one who should be serving her; that woman owes me an apology." And He seemed to say,

Oh, Joan, there is a bigger picture here. This is not about you. Trust me child, and please go serve Kim.

I would like to say that I followed God's prompting with a cheerful heart, but I was not the least bit enthusiastic about His directive. Exasperated, I marched off to the kitchen and grabbed an ice-cold glass out of the freezer. I wrapped it with a white paper napkin, filled it with ice cubes and fresh water and placed a slice of lemon on the rim. It looked beautiful, like something that would be served at an elegant restaurant. (I was so mad and hurt at the time that I'm glad it didn't cross my mind to spit in it until much later.)

I walked to her station and quietly said, "Here Kim, I thought you might like a glass of ice cold water. I know how hard you work. You're on your feet all day long, and I appreciate everything that you do." She looked at me eyes wide, mouth open. It must have been difficult to fathom that the woman she'd just kicked like an old dog was standing in front of her with a gift in hand. I could see the shame on her face. She was visibly shaken. I set the glass down and quietly walked away.

At the end of the day, I saw her slowly shuffling towards the exit door, her head hung low. It looked as if she carried the weight of the world upon her shoulders. By the grace of God and that alone, I walked over to her, put my arm around her shoulder, and softly said, "Oh Kim, I'm so sorry for that mix-up we had earlier today." She looked at me with the saddest of eyes and somberly replied, "I'm sorry, too."

In that hushed and holy moment, I sensed God saying to me, *Joan, because of your obedience today, you just allowed someone who does not know the depth of my love for her to experience my grace through you.* That thought brought me to my knees; it poured over me like warm healing waters. I was so thankful that God helped me put my wounded pride aside so that Kim could experience God's grace, His forgiveness, and His love.

It was an enormous lesson for me. On that eventful day I learned that life is always so much bigger than the immediate picture. I learned that no matter how terrible something may seem, there is typically something monumental at stake—something eternal going on in the life of the other person. And, if I'm willing to get on board with whatever God is doing, then I get to play a role in the grandest narrative of all... *His story.* What an honor it is when God invites us to be a part of anything that He is doing!

STEPPIN' OFF THE SIDEWALK

When we walk through an open door that God places before us we do not know what the outcome will be, because we walk by faith and not by sight. We walk not knowing what the next bend in the road may bring; only God knows that. Our responsibility is simply to listen for His lead, then follow and obey.

When I walked into Babylon on that cold February morning I had no idea that I was walking into my calling, a beautiful partnership with God for the mending of hearts in that broken world. There were so many precious people, with real stories and deep hurts. How was I supposed to connect with folks who did not know me or share my spiritual beliefs? I didn't know. Yet there in the midst of that eclectic group of individuals, there could be no denying that I sensed God seriously loved those people—and more to the point, He wanted me to show them just how much He truly loved them. I wasn't sure how to accomplish that undertaking.

God began to teach me not to beat them up with a Bible. They didn't need that; no one does. They were indisputably special to Him—it didn't matter if they knew Him or not! They were special because they were created in His image. And if they were special to Him, they needed to be special to me regardless of where they stood spiritually, politically, or morally.

While trying to figure out how to show (not just tell) the love of God to others, I stumbled upon the story of Desmond Tutu and the reason he became an Anglican Priest.

When Tutu was nine years old, he and his mother were walking down the street. A tall white man dressed in a black suit came towards them. In the days of apartheid, when a black person and a white person met while walking on a footpath, the black person was expected to step into the gutter to allow the white person to pass and nod their head as a gesture of respect. But this day, before a young Tutu and his mother could step off the sidewalk, the white man stepped off the sidewalk and, as Desmond and his mother passed, he tipped his hat in a gesture of respect to her!

Tutu had never seen anything like that before. When he asked his mother why that white man had stepped off the sidewalk, she told him that the man was an Anglican priest. He stepped off the sidewalk—because he was a man of God. Desmond decided there and then that he wanted to be an Anglican priest too. And what is more, he said he wanted to be a man of God.[41]

Reading the story of Desmond Tutu's defining moment was a defining moment for me. I knew that God was asking me to step off the sidewalk and let love lead the way. He was asking me to serve my co-workers, but what I didn't know was that in serving them, God was giving me their hearts and He was preparing me for a significant leadership role. The thought of a significant leadership role had never crossed my mind. Why would it? I had never been a leader, at least not in the way that corporate America defines leadership. The only people I had ever led were my two precious kids.

Because I knew He had said to step off the sidewalk for these people, I started looking for anything I could do to show honor and respect, bring a little joy and laughter into their world, and share in their burdens wherever I could. Then one day, six months into my job as Client Appointment Coordinator, the Salon and Spa Director handed in her resignation out of the blue. As quick as a snap, the CEO appointed me as her replacement!

I'll be honest: I didn't think I could do the job. I had never fired or hired anyone; led a team of people; implemented systems, policies and procedures; or even read a profit and loss statement. I told the CEO, "I'll be happy to be someone's assistant or right hand, but I don't think I can be the director." She said to me, "Tag, you're it!" And then, that team of people I had taken the time to get to know rallied behind *me*, a completely green leader who knew nothing about running an organization. Because I had looked for ways to step off the sidewalk and show them love, instead of offering clichés and talking points, they trusted me to lead them. They even allowed me to push them hard, and together we achieved things we never thought possible.

TRUTH

People flourish when they are loved. They will go above and beyond, and be willing to try new things. They will follow a loving leader into the fray and fight as hard as they can for a victorious outcome. It's time to bring love back into the work-force. Step off the sidewalk and create a culture of sacrificial teamwork, then watch and see the strength it brings to the organization you serve. Love changes everything!

Chapter Eight

Being People-Promoters and Confidence-Creators

*"Wherever you are, be all there! Live to the hilt
every situation you believe to be the will of God."*

Jim Elliot

We all long to know that our lives matter. We want to know that when its all been said and done, the life we lived made a difference in someone's life—even if it's just one person. Sadly, most people will never make the connection that work was meant to be a place where their unique gifts and talents could not only get the job done, but would impact the lives of others in profound and meaningful ways.

I saw this beautifully illustrated when my father passed away. The men and women who showed up for his funeral—fellow coworkers—did not speak about what a great worker he was; they spoke about a man who impacted their lives through his kindness and compassion. I had no idea that my father was loved by so many—people he had profoundly impacted through his ordinary work. Dad was not a scholar, a doctor, or a scientist making gigantic discoveries; he was just an everyday salesman who chose to bless the lives of those who shared his days. He found meaning and purpose in the work of his hands. I pray you will too. So keep reading, and may your heart be inspired to become the best on-the-job difference-maker this world has ever seen.

ALL YOU'VE GOT IS TODAY

When I stepped into my role as the Salon and Spa Director, I was so green it was ridiculous. Honestly, half the time I didn't know what I was doing. If that amazing team of people hadn't taken me under their wings and taught me the salon and spa business from the ground up, I never would have made it. Talk about being at the right place at the right time! I stumbled into my calling, and I was surrounded by great people who were gracious enough to help me learn. Without them, the leader in me might never have emerged.

In those beginning days, every day felt like a marathon. Exhaustion was my new normal. On any given day you could find me up to my ears scrambling to learn the business: how to read financials, interpret our service and retail analytics, set goals and get buy-in, launch promotional and marketing campaigns, create purchase orders, manage inventory, input staff schedules, oversee department meetings, grow our vendor relations, mediate conflict resolutions, and so on and so on. I was overwhelmed. But mostly, I didn't know how I was going to keep everyone happy. In a commission-based business, happiness is vital. I needed a game plan.

As I was dashing into work one morning, tired before the day even began (the kind of tired no amount of caffeine could fix), I slowed my pace just long enough to catch my breath. In that brief, unhurried minute, inhaling the sweet smell of the morning dew, I heard a familiar voice. It was His voice. (It may sound trite, but it's the truth. The book of John says, "My sheep hear my voice, and I know them and they follow Me" (Jn 10:27 ESV), and I know His voice!) He was saying, *One day at a time, dear child. All you've got is today. Tomorrow has not been promised. Today has enough worries of its own, so let go of tomorrow. Focus on today* (Matt 6:34).

You know, it's one thing to hear a well-known adage, but it's another thing to finally understand it. Like a light bulb going off in my head, I realized He was right—tomorrow might never come. Every day, people leave their homes, get in their cars, and head off to work, never to return home. We don't know when our last day on earth will be. We assume we will all be here tomorrow, but that's a false assumption. All we have is today, and that's enough.

I now had a game plan. "One Day at a Time" became my mantra, and a huge weight rolled off of my shoulders. If all I had was today, then by golly, I needed to make it count. For me, that meant being fully present in each moment, not distracted by tomorrow's worries. It dawned on me that there was only so much I could do in any given day. What mattered most was how I did those things. Did I do them with love? Did I show kindness to others? Did I make time for those in need of a helping hand? In learning to live one day at a time, my priorities as a leader were set—people first, paperwork second.

EMPTY CHAIR CONVERSATIONS

I wished I could say I mastered the mantra every single day, but I didn't. Some days I got it right, some days I didn't, and most days I needed to be reminded that people were more important than any paperwork I had sitting on my desk. Heck, we were in the people business. So, if I had any staff members who were falling apart, I had to stop whatever I was doing and listen to their concerns, their worries, their fears, and their frustrations.

I needed to help them pull themselves up by the bootstraps, so they could find a bit of hope, see the meaning behind their work, and go back to doing what they did best: providing an over-the-top luxurious experience for our guests. My priority had to be my staff. If my staff were happy, our guests were happy. It was that simple.

I don't know how I came up with the idea of placing an empty chair right next to my desk, but it worked! That empty chair served as a constant reminder that if God was never too busy for me, then I should never be too busy for my staff. It was also a visual invitation to my team.

Thinking about the transformational conversations that took place because of that chair makes me smile to this day. I can still see my team's faces—every one of them—the laughter, the tears, the shared cups of coffee as we swapped stories. We opened up our hearts to one another, dropped our defenses, took some risks, and worked through our problems, whether personal or professional. In making time for those who worked alongside me, I developed a leadership style that walked me into a meaningful life doing meaningful work.

You know, Saint Francis of Assisi used to say, "Preach the Gospel as much a possible, if necessary use words." Well, I think he was on to something. People want to see your walk before they hear you talk. If they cannot see love in the way you deal with people, then why in the world would they pay attention to your words? Leadership guru, John Maxwell, puts it this way, "people don't care how much you know until they know how much you care. There are three questions anyone will need answered before they will follow your lead—do you care for me? [. . .] can you help me? [. . .] and can I trust you?" An affirmative answer to those three questions will lead you into your best working days ever—and the opportunity to partner with God in the mending of hearts in a very broken world.

There is nothing better than seeing others find their wings and learn to fly. There was an amazing young man who worked for me. He was incredibly talented, and a compassionate soul with a smile as big as Texas and eyes that could light up the world. But in his early childhood he had been emotionally wounded, and he carried those scars deep within his heart into in adult life. No amount of therapy could erase the damage that had been done. Behind his smile and those bright eyes was a broken heart.

One day he asked me "Could we do lunch?" We set a date, and on that day we shared a simple meal and an extraordinary conversation. He opened up his life to me and unfolded his story between his shoulder shaking sobs. I wept, too, as he retraced the hurts he had suffered. Life had been so cruel to him. Though my hurts were not like his—his were so much deeper—in that moment, I was grateful that I too had struggled to overcome the stranglehold of depression on my life. I shared with him a little of my story so he would know I understood his pain and would pass no judgment. I talked about the dark places I had been and how I moved from darkness into the light of God's great love. In the sharing of our stories, a door of hope was opened and trust was invited in.

More and more that sweet boy made his way to the empty chair beside my desk. One day he just sat down, bowed his head low and began to cry. He steadied himself just a bit, and then looked me in the eyes and asked, "Do you think I'm going to make it?" I don't know what came over me, but in that moment I didn't care one iota about being politically correct, or being accused of being too Christian on the job. All I knew was that boy needed a strong dose of encouragement. He needed a friend, right then and there! Nothing was more important than his emotional well-being and the mending of his broken heart.

As I stopped what I was doing and took him by the hand, a boldness entered my spirit. I looked him square in eyes and said to him, "Oh darlin', I know you are going to make it. I'm praying for you. Others are praying for you. God is not going to let you go—you are going to make it!" I cannot explain it, but the words that flew out of my mouth were spoken with such authority that I knew they were not my words . . . they were God's. I knew that boy felt their power, because when he stood up, he squared his shoulders, held his head high and walked away with a determination in his steps. I think perhaps for the first time ever, that boy knew that Jesus, Friend of Sinners, was waging a war on his behalf and he was not alone.

I sat there at my desk, pondering what had just happened. I was blown away. Then I heard a familiar voice speak: *That, my child, is sacred work in a secular place.* I whispered back, "God, are these the stories that you want me to share with other believers?" *Yes,* He replied. *I want believers to recognize that their workplace is a platform that I have given them for my glory. Share these stories and encourage their hearts—their greatest days are still ahead.*

NEVER LEAVE 'EM BLEEDING

In that one moment, I finally got it. Work becomes infused with meaning and purpose when we invest ourselves into the lives of those around us. That sweet boy was just the tip of the iceberg.

People are broken, hurting and disengaged in their places of work. Never before has there been such a great need for love in the workplace. I'm not talking about love as a mushy emotion; I'm talking about love as a verb—an action that benefits another. This type of love can be performed by anyone; no title or position is needed. However, should you find yourself in a position of authority, be the kind of the leader you would want to follow. Lead by example. When it's time to burn the midnight oil, burn it with them. When it's time to go the extra mile, go two. Be the kind of leader people want to follow.

One of the greatest lessons I ever learned about leadership was about correction in the workplace. In my opinion, correction is rarely done well, and it's a major contributing factor in people's frustration at work.

No one possesses all knowledge. No matter how much we know, there will always be things that we do not know, things to be learned, and things to be improved upon. Correction is the way we learn and it is the way of life. Yet, more often than not, it is viewed as something to be feared. Most of the time, when someone is called into the boss's office and handed a write-up, the one on the receiving end is devastated. I've seen over and over again: the corrected individual is left bleeding on the floor with their heart ripped open, with no one to step in to offer restoration.

But correction doesn't have to be something to be feared! It can be wonderful if done properly. There was a time I was called into my boss's office. I don't even remember what I had done wrong, because the content of the conversation was not my takeaway. Here's what stuck with me: the way my boss spoke to me was so kind and affirming that I walked away feeling like I could conquer the world. I remember thinking, *If that's correction, I want more!* He helped me to see that correction was the way of life, not death, and that it was for my good! Because he chose to correct me lovingly, my defenses dropped and I could receive his valuable insight.

Shortly thereafter, another leader I served under shared something with me that I have never forgotten. He said, "You should never rebuke someone, unless in the same breath you can restore them." As the Salon and Spa director, I was eager to pass this advice on to others. One time, a newly-appointed front desk supervisor walked into my office, informing me that he was going to write up one of his subordinates. It was obvious that his new position had gone to his head just a little bit. I smiled at him, patted that empty chair, and said, "Have a seat."

I asked him, "What is your restoration plan?" The blank look on his face told me everything I needed to know. First, he did not know the purpose of correction. Second, he had probably never experienced correction with the goal of restoration. More than likely, he had only ever received crushing correction.

As our conversation continued, I shared with him the same wisdom that had been shared with me: "You should never rebuke someone, unless in the same breath you can restore them." I continued, "In this company, we don't correct anyone unless we can offer a restoration plan. If you don't have one, hand me the write-up, and *I* will do it, not you. We never leave our people bleeding on the floor with their hearts ripped open for all the world to see."

I looked at him and said, "We both know there can be difficult employees—employees that will drive you up the ever-loving wall. They will push every button you have. So, when I have someone sitting in my office, especially if it's that kind of employee, the first thing I do is look them in the eyes and remind myself that that person sitting in the hot seat is someone's child. And then I ask myself, if this were my child and they were sitting in their boss's office, in the hot seat, how would I want them to be treated? I would want that boss to see in them what I see. I would want that boss to believe in them enough to offer a way forward, a restoration plan. I would want that boss to come alongside them, the way my boss did years ago, and affirm his or her belief in them and their unlimited potential. That's what I do. I remind myself that there is inherent value in them because they are made in the image of God and they are special to someone . . . therefore, they should be special to me."

It is unfortunate that most people never receive this kind of correction. But I'm telling you, this was a game changer in my leadership approach. Now, I am not so naïve as to believe that everyone will accept the correction and make the necessary changes. But, more often than not, people are extremely grateful to be treated in a way that pairs correction with restoration. I have witnessed the hidden potential within others materialize into true talent once the fear of correction has been removed.

It's a different story when the individual rejects the restoration plan. At that point, I simply say, "It's obvious that this is not your cup of tea, so it's time for you to find employment elsewhere." I have no problem letting someone go when I know I did everything in my power to offer restoration. If they reject it, it's time to let that person go: they will never be the kind of employee who works for the good of all.

TRUTH

You really *can* love your work! Life is busy and life is messy, but choosing to embrace life, one day at a time, slows us down long enough to remind us of what is truly important—the people in our lives. "A 2005 study of terminal cancer patients found that, once the patients finished talking about their families, some of their most meaningful experiences involved doing work that mattered with people they cared about."[42] Seek to add value to the lives of those who fall within your circle of influence, and your days will never cease to be filled with a sense of meaning and purpose.

CHAPTER NINE

BEING BENEVOLENCE-BESTOWERS AND MEMORY-MAKERS

"We make a living by what we get.
We make a life by what we give."

Winston Churchill

The people we work with need so much more from us than mere words. They need to see the love of God in action through our deeds. If we are going to be difference-makers, then the time for talking is long past. I chose to open the door of my life and share my world so others might know God as I knew Him—as Father, Friend, and Redeemer of all I have ever screwed up.

MAMA BEAR LOVE

I believe in people with all my heart and I believe in second chances. Shoot, I'm a product of second chances! The best of me was developed and brought to life because I had people in my corner who wouldn't give up on me. Gosh, I'm glad they fought for me. Everyone, at one point or another, has needed an opportunity to make something right. Having been on the receiving end of those opportunities made me an advocate for second chances in the workplace. Nonetheless, sometimes my patience was pushed to the limits and I needed a reminder to stick with my convictions and extend a second chance even when I was madder than a wet hen.

The front desk staff buzzed my office, interrupting my work. "Ms. Joan, would you please come to the check-in counter?" I put down what I was working on and went to see what was the matter. With one look at their faces, I knew—he was late again. Something snapped inside of me and I was done. How many times had we gone round and round about his tardiness? I loved that young man, but this was it. He had just gone too far. He had crossed the line one too many times. My front desk staff were at the ever-lovin' end of their rope, demanding I take action.

I called his number . . . no answer. I called it again . . . still no answer. Then I remembered one time that he had been really ill—several-ambulance-trips-to-the-hospital ill—and my mama bear mode kicked into high gear. I pulled his personnel file, wrote down his home address, raced to my car, and shot out of the parking lot like a bat out of hell. I kept calling . . . no answer. I was frantic. He lived alone. What if something bad had happened? My mind imagined the worst-case scenario.

You see, tardiness and all, I loved that young man. He held a special place in my heart, and more than anything in the world I wanted him to succeed. He could cut, color, and style hair like nobody's business. He had everything in him to be a superstar, six-figure stylist. But, no matter how much I loved him, he was always late, and now had me scared me half to death. It was just too much.

I just wanted to see his face, to make sure he was okay. As I pulled into the apartment parking lot, my phone rang. I looked at the number: it was him. I answered the phone. "Joan?" he said. In the sternest of voices I replied, "Young man, where are you?"

He said, "I'm at the salon." I lit into him like a wild cat: "This is it. You've crossed the line. I am pulling up to your apartment right now. I was prepared to have the manager break down your door! I thought I was going find you dead! I will talk to you when I get back to the salon . . . but I've *had* it." I hung up the phone. I was shaking all over.

Everyone knew I had raced out of the salon to find my missing cub. You could have heard a pin drop when I walked back through the doors of the salon. All eyes were on me. I knew what I was going to do, but then someone interceded on that boy's behalf—someone from whom I least expected it.

Maureen, his no-nonsense department head, met me at the door. She quietly asked, "Are you mad? Are you going to fire him?" I replied, "I don't know, why do you ask?" I tried to be nonchalant, but I couldn't hide my irritation. She said, "Oh Joan, I didn't know his story; I didn't know what was going on! I'm asking you to please give him a second chance!" I smirked at her and said, "What? 'Merciless Maureen' is asking me to extend grace? What's going on?" She said, "Joan, just talk to him. He needs a second chance."

I headed to my office. Out of the corner of my eye, I saw him standing off to the side. I could see the stress on his face, and I'm sure he could see the irritation on mine. I turned, looked him straight in the eyes, and said in a not-so-pleasant tone, "Come with me." I opened the door to my office and he walked as far away from me as he could get (a good five or six feet). As he turned to face me, he defensively crossed his arms over his chest. He just knew this was it. I was going to send him packing.

The battle lines were drawn. He stood on one end of the long, narrow room, and I stood on the other. He towered over me at least a foot and half. (I used to call him my gentle giant. If he had had a mind to, he could have crushed me.) He didn't say a word. I was staring at the floor, thinking about Maureen's plea: *I'm asking you to please give him a second chance!*

I lifted my head, looked him in the eyes, and said, "I only have one thing to say." Then I opened my arms as wide as I could. That gentle giant walked over and fell into my arms, and we cried and cried and cried some more. It was the most beautiful moment I have ever experienced in the workplace. When we finally composed ourselves, I said, "I thought you were dead! I was so worried. Now, tell me what's going on." He told me the story, and it was heartbreaking. No *wonder* he was having a hard time focusing. As painful as it was to tell me, it broke something off of him, like a release from his chains. It was a fresh start for both of us. After that, he gave it his best effort and is now a successful, high-profile stylist. I'm so glad Maureen implored me to give him a second chance.

ON BEING INTENTIONAL

In making a decision to be a difference-maker, my heart was opened to more than I ever thought possible. Together, my team and I built a culture of pouring into one another and of caring for our fellow co-workers. It wasn't a perfect environment, but it was a compassionate environment: an environment that was willing to listen and, when warranted, extend second chances. (Did we fire people? Yes, but only people unwilling to honor others or accept correction and restoration.)

The loving habits I formed at work spilled into my personal life and made me a better person. I was challenged on so many levels to live out my faith among people whose personal beliefs and convictions differed wildly from mine. When you get to know someone with different beliefs, you begin to see them in a different light. They become more real to you: their sorrow makes you sad, their tears make you cry, their laughter makes you smile, and the twinkle in their eyes makes you want to find a way to connect. You find a way to hold on to your convictions and still love them in the process.

I hired people who were different from me. I hired people who were incredibly talented. I hired people who other salons rejected simply because I felt a familiar nudge that it was the right thing to do. Then, I spent time getting to know them. As we worked side by side, sharing life in the workplace, I deliberately created memory-making moments. Yeah, you read that right—memory-making moments with my co-workers! Creating those moments became a strategic part of the way I lead and loved my team. Why was it important to create those magical moments?

Well, here's the deal: most people cannot change overnight. None of us became who we are today with a snap of the fingers. It took a lifetime of some good moments and some really awful ones. I've never met anyone who didn't have a few battle scars. Trust has to be earned in every single relationship, and it takes time. However, when we choose to invest our time, trust grows exponentially. Every shared cup of coffee and conversation becomes a memory-making moment. We may not see immediate healing in someone's brokenness, but I can promise you this: when the time is right, they will remember the one who loved them just as they were. They will remember that shared cup of coffee where friendship grew and trust began.

It's a given that on the road ahead, all of us will encounter sorrow and heartbreak. But I believe that, when sadness comes, the people I made memories with will look back on our conversations, and come to a place to receive His love in ways they never could have before. They will remember those who loved them well. I'm telling you, we may never know the full impact of those moments until we're on the other side.

I remember sharing a life-changing conversation with my assistant. We were just doing everyday work stuff, nothing out of the ordinary, but we were enjoying each other's company, so we chatted away about nothing in particular. Then, the conversation slowed and he said to me, "You know Ms. Joan, last night my partner asked me, 'Why do you share everything with Ms. Joan?

What's the big deal?'" (Now that boy had the most adorable smile; he was like sunshine on rainy day.) He glanced at me with that sweet face and said, "I told him, 'When I talk with Ms. Joan, it's sort of like talking with Jesus.'" I thought my heart would stop. Never in my life had anyone said something like that to me. Those words changed my life. I became instantly aware of the power of my words.

When we engage in memory-making moments, we come to think about others differently, and are often moved with compassion to not only pray for those we work alongside, but to communicate with them in ways that affirm their significance and allow God's love to shine on them.

COMMON GROUND

There were staff members at the salon who were not like me, yet we cared deeply for one another. Love has a way of finding common ground even when political and spiritual views may differ. When I opened my heart to my co-workers, I made a decision to open my home as well. One of my all-time favorite memory-making moments was hosting a dinner party for several co-workers and their partners. The meal was great, but the company and the conversation were even better.

After the meal was over, we moved into the family room and talked for hours. It was long into the night before we said our goodbyes. When we finally did, my family and I were humbled by the power of love that flowed into our home that night. We felt His presence and sensed His joy . . . simply because we threw open the doors and invited love to reign.

Those memory-making moments create an environment where people can respectfully disagree without losing love for one another. I am smiling even as I write these words, because another memory is flashing back. Jimmy, Randall, and I were standing in the middle of the salon, arguing—well, respectfully disagreeing—about some differences in belief when all of a sudden Jimmy raised his hands in a dismissive wave. With the biggest grin ever, he looked at me and said, "Oh, Joan, we know what you believe." I replied, with both hands opened wide, "And?" There was a slight pause, then another broad grin and the simple reply, "But we know that you love us!"

That made my day! I had come full circle. I had walked into Babylon uncertain of my future and not knowing how in the world I could possibly connect with so many different people I had so little in common with. Yet, there in the midst of that melting pot of colorful people I found meaningful work infused with passion and purpose. In the process I also discovered that you can absolutely learn to live with your convictions, not compromise your core beliefs, and still form precious friendships with those who hold differing opinions.

TRUTH

If the people you work with aren't church-going folk, then chances are they never will be. They might never experience the transformational love of God unless you bring the church to them. Opening our home and inviting people in to share a meal with our family not only impacted our guests; our hearts overflowed with unexplainable joy. I think all of Heaven rejoiced over that shared meal. Nothing has impacted our lives more than letting down our walls and loving people right where they are . . . and then trusting God to move in their lives.

E.M Bounds once said, "Talking to men for God is a great thing, but talking to God for men is greater still."[43] I can tell you this: sharing God's love by sharing your home will grow your prayer life immensely. Because when you get to know people's heartaches you cannot help but be compelled to lift up their sorrow and suffering to the only One who can put their lives back together again. Want to be an impactful on-the-job difference-maker? Look around and see who God puts on your heart, then invite them to share a meal. You will never be the same—and you will know that you are indeed partnering with God in the mending of hearts in this broken world.

PART FOUR

WORK STRATEGY:
THERE WILL BE BATTLES,
BUT GOD WILL WIN

I hated work, but then I discovered that God loved it, and that He was a worker himself! More astonishing than that, He wanted me to partner with Him! Saying "yes" to God's invitation to be a difference-maker doesn't mean I've never faced fear or experienced disappointment. No, I believe every Christian will face those things, and even more. Saying "yes" to the call of God make us a target for the enemy.

There will be battles, and you will get wounded. Some days, your heart will feel like it's been broken in a million pieces. And when those days come, hold fast to your Deliverer and remember this: your destiny, sweet child of God, is never in the hands of man. God alone holds your destiny safely in the palm of His nail-scarred hands.

I have been blindsided, betrayed, falsely accused, lied to, and cursed at, and I'm still here. I survived, and so will you. In fact, I can almost guarantee that with every heartbreak, you will emerge a better person and a stronger believer, unshakable in your convictions and shining so brightly that the devil will be sorry he messed with you. Do you doubt this? I promise you,

God wastes nothing of things you suffer. He is ever-faithful, and He will redeem them.

This last section is a collection of stories of wrongs suffered, yet redeemed. That's what God does. He makes all things beautiful. When you face those dark days, and you feel alone on the job, may these stories give you courage and remind you that your destiny is in the palm of God's hand. He placed you in your job, and no one can remove you unless God grants permission—and should that happen, God will walk you in to your next assignment. Do not fear! He has promised to never leave you or forsake you.

CHAPTER TEN
OH SNAP, WE HIRED JUDAS—
LOVE FOR A SEASON

*"To be a Christian means to forgive the inexcusable because
God has forgiven the inexcusable in you."*

C.S. Lewis

N ow you've come to understand that work was meant
to be a blessing and not a curse. You see that there
is no dichotomy between the sacred and the secular.
You've embraced your God-given platform and have become a
difference-maker in your place of employment. But then, you
encounter a Judas on the job. What are you gonna do? Well,
here's the deal: Jesus had his Judas, and you will too. It's the
nature of living in this fallen world. Let me share with you the
lesson I learned about leading and loving the Judas on the job.

BEAUTIFUL GIRL IN THE HOT PINK SHIRT

I was sitting behind a mountain of paperwork stacked high
upon my desk when I first saw the beautiful girl in the hot
pink shirt. I glanced over the rim of my bifocals and noted her

hourglass figure, gorgeous hair, and impeccable dress. She was a picture of femininity and grace. She had come to interview for an entry-level position. Though she looked a little nervous, she displayed an easy smile that seemed to speak of warmth and friendliness.

Her resume was very impressive. However, prior to the interview, our management team had asked why she applied for an entry-level position when, according to her resume, she was overqualified. That should have been a huge red flag, and we should have explored it thoroughly, but we didn't. We were under intense pressure to replace a high-performing stylist who had abruptly resigned, so we ignored our intuition.

The woman interviewed fantastically! She was charming, witty, and charismatic. She offered everything we were looking for, and *then* some! Carried away with her magnetic personality (and extremely embellished resume), we hired her on the spot. Not only did we hire her, we immediately promoted her to our elite team of stylists.

Had we insisted that she Earn The Right to be included on our team of highly educated professionals, as had been required of every member on that team, we would have discovered that she had rightly applied for an entry-level position. That gal had a lot to learn, including how to treat her peers. Nonetheless, with high hopes, we welcomed the charismatic, gorgeous lady in the hot pink shirt to our team of the most sought-after stylists in Houston.

It took less than a few weeks to recognize that we were in for a bumpy ride. She was lacking in many skills. She knew it and so did everyone else, but "teamwork" was not part of her vocabulary. Rather than endear herself to her teammates and humbly ask for help, she strutted about the place as if everyone was beneath her. It was awful. She cunningly pointed her finger at others, whispered behind everyone's back, and stirred the pot wherever she could. She treated her peers with sharp contempt and alienated herself from just about everybody. In circumventing the tried and true principle of Earn The Right, we created a mess.

Our Judas made enemies quicker than she could make friends. She was miserable, and she was hell-bent on making others miserable, too. The team was on pins and needles, and many were often in tears. She got on everyone's last nerve. I regretted the day we hired her. I hated what was happening . . . especially in my own heart. I couldn't recall a time I had ever harbored such feelings of resentment for anyone. Even though I smiled at her outwardly, inwardly I was full of anger and fury. She had brought dissension and disharmony into the salon, and I just wanted her to go away! I kept remembering the young woman we had interviewed—that charismatic, good-looking gal—and I couldn't help but wonder, *What went wrong?*

Then it hit me—we'd hired a Judas, a betrayer in our midst. I didn't know what to do. The thought of betrayal and the destruction that follows made me sick to my stomach. I thought about Jesus and wondered how He put up with His Judas, let alone love the man who would hand him over for crucifixion? In that moment, I wasn't one bit like Jesus. I had no love in my heart for this young woman. Moreover, I did *not* want to be crucified. Yet, I had a feeling that was exactly what was going to happen.

LOVE WITH CAPITAL A

In the midst of that terrible season, I was attending a marriage and family counseling class at The College of Biblical Studies. One night, during a class discussion, my dam of self-control burst. I shared with the class what I was dealing with, and then, in unbridled fury, all of my pent-up frustration spewed out like vomit. I blurted out, "Honestly, I think I hate this girl! She's making my life a living hell. She's the most un-teachable person I have ever known, she is a Judas in my midst and I will *not* be crucified by this twit of a woman!" I was horrified at the intensity of my anger. At that moment there was zero evidence of the love of God residing inside of me. I was so ashamed.

Thank God for divine intervention and for a wise course instructor who looked beyond my rage to see the pain in my heart. I had taken a hit on the battlefield of life, and I needed someone to carry me off the battlefield into the safety of my Father's love. Without a word of accusation or condemnation course instructor, Jacobi Lewis, walked to the whiteboard. He picked up the blue maker and drew a large capital A and a capital B on the board. All eyes were on Mr. Lewis when he turned to face me. He looked right at me and said, "Joan, I think I can help you."

Mr. Lewis asked me, "Do you believe God is sovereign?" I sulkily replied, "*Yes,* I believe God is sovereign." Then he said, "Well, if God is sovereign, then everyone who enters your life has been placed there by His hand. No one comes into your life by accident." He pointed to the capital A and B on the board and said, "Therefore, you will either be in an A or a B relationship with every person who enters your life."[44] The letter B stands for Builder. Let me ask you this: who can you build?" I responded, "Well, I can only build those who want to be built—those who are teachable." He responded, "Exactly!"

He went on to explain, "If you cannot be in a Builder relationship with someone, then your only option is an A relationship. In fact, if a B relationship is impossible, the only reason God sent her into your life was for an A relationship." So, I asked the inevitable question: "What does A stand for?"

Looking me square in the eyes, he said, "A stands for Ambassador of Love." He paused to let that thought sink in deeply, then proceeded, "This person who has caused you so much pain, God never intended you to fix. Right now, she's broken and unteachable. Don't even try to fix her—you can't! She was sent to you for one reason, and one reason only: that you might be an Ambassador of love to her. Stop trying to build her; that's not why she's in your life."

Mr. Lewis's compassionate voice broke the silence that hung in the room. "In fact, you should weep for this woman. She is probably lost and without hope. The condition of her soul should drive you to your knees on her behalf. You don't have to fix her; you just need to love her. Be that Ambassador of Love: it's the only reason God sent her into your life."

Those words changed everything, and the tears fell like raindrops. I wept for the beautiful girl in the hot pink shirt, and I wept with a heart full of gratitude for this fresh understanding. The anger, bitterness and frustration that had consumed me for months vanished instantly.

I knew what I had to do. I needed to ask for her forgiveness. As she entered the salon, when she walked past my desk, I reached out my hand and said, "Hey, I need to talk with you, could you sit down for just a minute?" I smiled at her and gestured to the empty chair beside my desk. I could tell she was skeptical and unsure, but reluctantly she sat down.

Quietly I said, "I need to ask your forgiveness. I have not given you the benefit of the doubt, nor have I taken the time to genuinely listen when you asked to be heard. For that, I am sorry. Please know that this empty chair is for you too. From now on, I promise that I will make time to listen. Will you please forgive me?"

I could see the shock and disbelief on her face, but I could also see relief. I continued, "I know there's been a wall between us, and that's on me, not you. I just want you to know, you are always welcome to this empty chair, and I will hear you out. I am sorry." She said, "I forgive you," and then we chatted about small stuff and shared a laugh or two, anything to move us forward and put the past behind us.

When I let go of the Builder responsibility and embraced the Ambassador opportunity, everything changed in our relationship.

I was free to love, not to fix, and she was freed to just be herself: a person in need of a little kindness and love. It was amazing how quickly the atmosphere shifted within the entire salon. It was especially delightful when a bouquet of hot pink flowers was hand-delivered to my desk by the girl in the hot pink shirt.

TRUTH

After that classroom discussion, I began to assess every relationship in the light of the Builder or Ambassador Principle. If it was possible to be a Builder for anyone I was asked to teach, coach or mentor, I spent time building them. However, if I discerned that I couldn't be a Builder in their lives, I let go of that role and assumed the role of Ambassador. Sometimes people were too broken to be pushed or coached, and they needed a healing season with an Ambassador of Love. Many times, that Ambassador season proved to be just what they needed to move into a Builder relationship.

There will be people in our lives who we cannot build. It doesn't matter why. What matters is that we recognize whether to spend our efforts building or simply loving. Spend your energy on those you can build, and spend your love on those you can't. Those who just need love will probably only be in your life for a short season. They will move on to other pastures, but they will always remember the love that impacted their lives for that one brief season.

Chapter Eleven

It's Not Equal, And It Never Will Be—Love Trumps All

"True love is about sacrifice for the sake of the ones you love"

Francis Chan

You've become an on-the-job difference-maker and you'd do just about anything for your team, your coworkers, or those within your sphere of influence. You're the sunshine on the job, the positive force behind every endeavor, the calm in the midst of other people's storms. But let's be honest: sometimes you wish that the love you lavish on others would be reciprocated every once in a while! That would be nice, but it's not likely. Difference-makers and love-leaders will always love more deeply. Let me explain.

NO COMPARISON

I was feeling a little blue and wishing that just once someone on my team would care about me as deeply as I cared for them, and that got me thinking about my mom. For as long as I could remember, mom had always been my best friend. I loved her and she loved me—period, end of story. I thought we shared an equal love right until the moment I held my first-born child. In that one glorious moment, I knew unequivocally that mom's love for me far surpassed any love I had ever held for her. There was no comparison, and there never would be.

Sitting at my desk, in the middle of my pity party, the memory of mom's love helped me to reconcile that, just as a mother's love runs deeper than that of a child's, so will the love of a difference-maker or a love-leader. A difference-maker's love will always run deeper than those they are called to serve. It's not equal, and it never will be. More importantly, just as a child tests the love of a parent, so a team member or a co-worker may, at times, test the love of a leader or an on-the-job difference-maker. You can bet your bottom dollar it will happen! However, accepting the fact that being a leader or a difference-maker was a lot like being a parent—that we're gonna love deeper and sacrifice more—helped me to be okay with the lack of reciprocal love and even the testing of that love. But it was a hard lesson to learn.

JUST WAIT 'TIL HE FINDS OUT

I was looking for a way to connect with Liam. He was our new hire, and I hadn't yet invested in some quality one-on-one time with him. I had an errand to run for the company, so, I asked him to come along. I thought it would be the perfect opportunity for small talk and the beginning of a meaningful work-related relationship. I couldn't have been more wrong. It was the most perplexing discussion I'd ever had, with consequences I never imagined.

I remember almost every word of our conversation. In my mind, I can still see us driving around the streets of Houston on that hot summer day when he launched into a diatribe about the Christians he had known. He did not like Christians, and the cynicism in his voice lead me to believe that he had experienced a good deal of hurt from the believers he had encountered. It made me sad. I, too, had often been hurt over the way some believers treated gay people. It made my heart sick.

I nodded my head, and continued to listen as he ranted and raged against Christianity in general. My goodness, what was this guy gonna do when he found out his new boss was a Christian? Would he believe I was sorry he'd had such bad experiences with Christians, and that I understood where he was coming from?

I got his anger, I really did. For a long time, I didn't know how to hold on to my biblical convictions and still embrace those who were opposed to them. I struggled long and hard to know what it meant to be in the world, but not of it (Jn 17:14-15). I confess that prior to gaining that understanding, I looked down my nose at others. Though it wasn't intentional, I know I gave off those vibes. But mercifully, my years in the salon world taught me that all men and women are loved by God . . . and if they are loved by God, they should be loved by me. Billy Graham's quote, "It is God's job to judge, the Holy Spirit's job to convict and my job to love," became how I strove to live my life.

But Liam did not personally know me, nor did he have any knowledge of my deeply-held belief. He had no way of knowing that he would be respected and appreciated, regardless of his sexuality or his robust opinions about Christians. The more he talked, the more I knew I needed to let him know that I was a Christian—and, moreover, that I understood why he felt the way he did.

So, when he slowed down long enough to catch his breath and let me get a word in edgewise, I simply said, "Liam, I am so sorry that has been your experience with other Christians. It makes me really sad because I'm a Christian." I continued, "I have many friends who don't share my beliefs. Some are straight, and some are gay. Some are black, and some are white. Some are Democrat, and some are Republican. We don't always see eye to eye, yet we are thick as thieves and friends indeed. Liam,

I can tell you this: come life or even death, no matter what my friends and I may face, we are friends first and we will stand together. In their darkest hours, regardless of our differences, they can count on me."

I think he was genuinely shocked to discover that I was a Christian, because he didn't say much after that and he kept the conversation really light. I honestly thought he grasped I was offering an olive branch, and that I was openly sorry that he had had such repulsive experiences with other Christians. I had no idea that the conversation we had shared totally offended him—nor did I have a clue how angry he was. But I was about to find out.

BLINDSIDED AND DUMBFOUNDED

Come the following business day, I got a clue as to just how offended Liam really was. I was notified that Liam wanted to file a grievance against me with my supervisor. I was blindsided and dumbfounded to say the least. I could not imagine what I had said to Liam that warranted a complaint. I mean, was he not listening? Did he not hear me talk about my precious friendships with those who held different political and religious views?

When I met with my boss, I shared with her the entire conversation from start to finish. I was hurt, I was flustered, and yes, I was irritated! It didn't make any sense to me. I thought, Did he not hear me tell him how much I adored my co-workers? I found it unthinkable that I was in a pickle simply because I responded in a gracious manner to Liam's opposition to Christianity. I looked at my boss and said, "Are you telling me an employee can share their opinions with me and I'm not allowed to respond with my opinion? Because if that's true, it doesn't seem right or fair."

I'll be honest—my first impulse was to fight back. None of my co-workers had ever accused me of anything, let alone filed a grievance against me! I needed to calm down, because it would not be pretty if I let this get the better of me and destroy everything I held dear. There was much at stake: most importantly, God's glory. I am so thankful that the Holy Spirit is our constant companion, and that He holds us close when we are unjustly targeted. I'm so thankful for God's intervention.

I silently prayed for grace, for wisdom, and most of all for God to show up and walk me through the nightmare. I took a deep breath, and then I stated the obvious: "It's clear that Liam did not understand the intent of my heart. But you know what, there is nothing I can do if he wants to file a complaint. Let him go ahead and file. My entire team will stand with me. All the people I have dearly loved for all these many years will testify on my behalf. My team knows how much I love them and they'll go the distance for me."

She agreed and quickly said, "You know, after hearing your side of the story, and knowing your heart and history with our team, I think you're right. I think he totally misunderstood the intent of your heart. What do you say to taking Liam out to lunch and clearing the air? Let's bring this out in the open and talk about this misunderstanding together." And that's exactly what we did. We took Liam to lunch and I am so glad we did. It was awkward, but so worth it.

As we shared a meal, the lunchtime discussion that ensued was open, honest, deep and quite remarkable. In hindsight, Liam was extremely gracious, given his history with people of faith who had been less than kind to him. I was able to share real-life stories with Liam and talk about the relationship I shared with my staff and what they meant to me. Liam agreed that he had not understood the intent of my heart, and we moved from his being offended to a cautious acceptance of my offer of friendship. And I was good with that—after all, trust can only be earned, not demanded. Liam needed time to understand the heart of a difference-maker.

BEAT UP AND BROKEN

I am very thankful that my boss chose to hear me out and to demonstrate her belief in me by fostering an environment where it was safe to be transparent, lay everything on the table and get to the heart of the matter. Because, unbeknownst to all of us, in just a few short weeks, Liam was going to need a really good friend: someone who would sincerely care about his well-being and be willing to express deep compassion.

A little more than a week or two after Liam and I had made our peace, I was working late one evening, alone in my office, when the phone rang. It was Liam—he was crying. He had been assaulted, severely beaten, and wanted to know if he could come to my office and speak with me.

I'll be honest, I was a little hesitant—nope, I was a lot hesitant. I had never had anyone file a complaint against me, and it had shaken me more than I let on. I was glad we had reconciled and that everything was okay between us, but I never wanted to experience that again. I didn't know if I was willing to put my heart on the line for Liam and risk being misunderstood or face another filed grievance. On the other hand, how could I possibly ignore his plea for help? I couldn't. Hadn't I just told him that his life mattered and that he could count on me because he was on my team?

Nonetheless, a battle broke out in my heart. A million thoughts sped through my brain in rapid-fire succession. This was risky. I was alone. There would be no witnesses. If he didn't like the outcome, he could say anything. He could file another grievance. I wondered to myself, Of all the people he could have reached out to, why did he want to see me? Suddenly, I remembered my mom's far-surpassing love, and I knew that this was a difference-maker moment. This was a moment to love even when that love had been severely tested. I got it. I understood what was a stake. So I told him, "Come on by, Liam, I'll be waiting for you."

A little while later he knocked softly on my door. Trying to keep it light, I casually said, "Come on in, my friend." He slowly peeked around the doorframe. His handsome face was battered and bruised. I put my hand over my mouth, and blinked back tears. My heart was overwhelmed. It took every ounce of self-control to not jump up, run around the desk, and wrap that boy in my arms. It was awful. I felt such hurt for him.

I could barely speak, so I motioned for him to take a seat as I gathered my composure. I had never seen someone so beaten up. He slumped into the chair and his eyes betrayed a sea of deep suffering. Finally, I whispered, "Oh, Liam, I am so sorry . . . my heart is hurting for you." I didn't know what else to say, so I paused for a moment and silence filled the room as the tears ran down his face.

I don't know what possessed me, but I blurted, "Liam, tell me about your mom. Does she hug you very much?" He sniffled, "Sometimes—yeah, sometimes she does." I said, "Well, right now, I think you need a hug and I'd like to give you one, but I'm afraid you might file a complaint." He started to weep and said, "Oh, Miss Joan, I could really use a hug right now." I don't advise this to people in positions of authority, but in that moment, I threw caution to the wind and just hugged the boy. He buried his head on my shoulder and let the tears fall. Oh, for grace to love more freely! I am so grateful to a God who has loved me well and entrusted others into my care.

Finally, he stepped away and eased his beat up body back into his chair. The room grew quiet and I gave him space to gather his thoughts and share them if he felt inclined to do so. He ventured to fill in a few details, but the ordeal was just too raw to even talk about. And I didn't really need the details. That's not why he sought me out. He just needed a friend.

I had to admit, it was kind of ironic. Only a few short weeks ago, Liam thought I was his enemy, and I thought he had it in for me. But God had other plans—plans for Liam to experience the Father's Love in a time of great need. As our conversation drew to an end, I looked over at Liam and mustered up the courage for one final blessing. I smiled at him and with a twinkle in my eyes said, "Liam, if it's not too much, I would really like to pray for you . . . but then again, I'm still afraid that you might file a complaint."

He looked over at me and tears welled in his eyes, and then he said, "I could really use your prayers, and I promise—no complaint will be filed." I reached across the desk, took his hands in mine, bowed my head, and prayed. I prayed that God would mend his wounded body and heal his broken heart. I prayed that Liam would know how much the Father loved him, that his life would be full of joy, and that the blessings of God would fall upon him all the days of his life.

When I finished praying, Liam looked at me and said, "Miss Joan, if the day ever comes that I am no longer working for you, should you meet me on the street, I hope you will stop and chat a while—because you have a friend in me." Considering the start of our relationship, nothing could have made my heart happier!

TRUTH

There will be moments on the job when we will need to be reminded that the love of a difference-maker or a love-leader should far surpass the love of those he or she is called to serve. It's not equal, and it never will be. Those we serve will sometimes test the love that we proclaim we have for others. For the most part, they will not test this love out of vengeance. More likely, it will be that they just need reassurance that you are who you say you are; and more importantly, that you genuinely care about their well-being.

CHAPTER TWELVE

SOMEONE'S GUNNING FOR MY JOB—LOVE YOUR COMPETITION

"Write injuries in the sand, kindnesses in stone."

Unknown

You've learned that you're either a builder or an ambassador in someone's life. You've learned that as a difference-maker, the love you have for others will sometimes be greater than the love they have for you. You've stayed the course and burned brightly for God's glory. You love your job more than ever, and you love your teammates too. But now, someone is gunning for your job and wants to oust you from your position. Another battle, another target on your back. This time it's not just someone; it's a teammate and a couple of higher-ups looking to push you right out the door forever. So what are you gonna do? Well, listen up, 'cause I've got a story for you!

A BITTER PILL TO SWALLOW

Three times someone has gunned for my job. The first time it happened, I completely blew it. I resigned my position and let it be known I was leaving because of that son of a gun who wanted to steal my job! I wasn't gonna put up with the pettiness. It was awful and my behavior gained me absolutely nothing but heartache. The second time, proved to be a blessing in disguise: it became a foundational lesson on how to beat the devil at his own game and win a friend in the process!

The third time around was the same lesson as the second—how to beat the devil at his own game. However, the third time was much more challenging because I'd finally fallen in love with my work and co-workers. I had much more to lose. In addition, that third time included betrayal—humiliation and demotion.

The betrayal was hard to overlook because they undermined the root of trust, and everything goes to hell in a hand basket without trust. It was hard to withstand that third round of someone gunning for my job. Though I overcame that difficult challenge, let me be absolutely clear: I can take no credit for surviving that horrible ordeal. The credit goes to God.

Without a supernatural intervention—an impartation of His divine grace—there's no way in Hades that I would have endured the disgrace of humiliation and demotion that were placed upon me as a condition of continued employment. God kept my feet firmly planted on the platform that He had given me, because in actuality, I wanted to run away and never come back. So here's what happened.

LEADERSHIP SHAKEUP

In 2010, a new leadership team was slated to take the helm and steer our organization into a bright new future. Several months prior to the scheduled official transition date, I had been invited to a private meeting where it was inferred that I would be promoted to the key leadership position in order to ensure a successful changeover. It was a position I would have been honored to hold. More importantly, it was a position my team would have supported in an effort to forge strong relationships with the new leadership.

However, that's not what transpired. Only weeks out from transition day, all key players were gathered around the table, hashing out the final details, when the leadership team stated that a younger, thinner, and prettier person would be appointed to the key leadership role they had inferred would be given to me. They believed that the younger appointee better suited the new direction of our company and they sure hoped that there would be no hard feelings.

No hard feelings? They had just publicly passed me over, and they didn't respect me enough to privately inform me that they would be withdrawing their offer of promotion. What did they expect, that I'd jump for joy? It felt like a slap in the face!

To make matters even worse, someone I trusted completely not only *knew* what was going to go down at the meeting, but had initiated the promotion of the younger appointee over me. I didn't say a word for the rest of the meeting. I sat there, crumbling inside, not believing what had just happened. I genuinely didn't know what my next step would be. I didn't know if I had it in me to stick around. Broken promises, let alone the humiliation and betrayal, made me doubt everything and everyone.

Fortunately, I didn't fly off the handle and quit. I decided to walk that conflict out one day at a time and see what would unfold. As the transition day approached and the announcement was made that Hannah would be promoted to the position of Director of Operations, and that I would hold the position of General Manager (a title change only/no promotion) bewilderment was written all over my team's faces. They didn't understand this decision, and they wondered if I was okay with the new changes.

There wasn't anything I could do to change what had been decided, so I had kept my feelings hidden to all but a few. I was in a hard place because I loved my job and I loved my coworkers. They were the best group of people ever, but I had been passed over and betrayed and hurt was raging inside of me. Then, in the middle of that bitter setback—something extraordinary happened.

As my teammates asked questions and voiced their concerns over the new roles and titles, I can't explain what happened other than to tell you that God divinely intervened in the moment. With every question asked, I found myself smoothing things over and assuring my team, "Everything is gonna be okay. Yeah, it's a little bittersweet, but bittersweet is good . . . no, bittersweet is great!"

My mind fixated on the word "bittersweet." Oh yes, being passed over and betrayed was a bitter pill to swallow. But on the other hand, there was God's insanely sweet love for Hannah… instantly, in that moment, I knew Hannah was not my enemy— she was my friend.

God supernaturally stirred up within me a deep well of compassion for Hannah. There is no other explanation for the sudden change in my heart. I'm not that bighearted, not that compassionate, and not all that forgiving. What I experienced that day can only be attributed to God's divine grace.

TELLING IT LIKE IT IS

Here's the deal, nothing was fair about what had happened and that's really neither here nor there. It happened. Someone whispered in the ears of the leadership team to consider Hannah for that key position. Private meetings were held and decisions were made, but no one told me anything until that eventful day when the leadership team simply announced that a younger appointee would be better suited for that position.

Did Hannah know what would be announced in that meeting? Yes, I'm sure she did. But I do not fault her. She was presented with an opportunity to take on a significant leadership role and why should she not try her hand in leading a fantastic group of people? If the roles were reversed I am sure I would have stepped up to the plate and accepted the position too.

Hannah was as smart as a whip, knock-down gorgeous, and just a great gal all around. The only problem was that within the organization she had never led more than a handful of people. She needed time to grow into the significant role she had been given—time to forge relationships with team members she did not know.

On the first day in her new position, Hannah and I went to lunch and I decided then and there to just shoot straight with her. As the meal was served, I looked over at her and said,

"I'm just gonna tell it like it is—at least the way I see it. You and I both know the job should have been mine. But that's not what happened."

I then went on to state the obvious:

"I lead a hundred people or more on a daily basis. You lead a team of seven, maybe eight. I oversee one hundred and fifty purchase orders or more per month. And you, no more than fifteen. I direct eight departments; you direct three. You have never shouldered a load this big within this organization. But here's the deal: I'm here to tell you that I'm not your enemy, and I will be your friend. I will help you every step of the way. Hannah, you are so loved by God and He has told me to come alongside of you and *help* you, not hinder you. And that's exactly what I'm gonna do. Whatever you need, I'm on your side."

I loved Hannah (still do). Given time, she would have made a great Director of Operations. However, the newly installed leadership team was also in a time of learning. There was a learning curve for everyone involved. In that process of learning, not all of the personalities meshed together well. Eventually, Hannah moved on to another company, where she has absolutely flourished and enjoyed great success. I am thrilled for Hannah and the success she has achieved. It was an honor to be her friend, and together we beat the devil at his own game.

You know, there's a story in the Bible that gave me great courage to do the right thing, in the middle of the pain and betrayal and someone gunning for my job. It's the story of Jonathan, son of Saul, King of Israel. Jonathan was heir to the throne of Israel, next in line to rule the nation. But his father Saul blew it with God, and God handed over the kingdom of Israel to David, a lowly shepherd boy. Jonathan comprehended that he had been passed over, he would not be king, and that God had appointed David as the future ruler of Israel.

Now here's the beautiful part, the real lesson. Rather than get mad and throw a hissy fit, Jonathan aligned his heart with God and made David his dearest friend, not his enemy. He trusted God and threw in his support for David. Whenever it was in Jonathan's power to help David, he did so with all his heart. He embraced his competition as friend rather than a foe and became the dearest friend David had ever known.

Even as a difference-maker—well, especially as a difference-maker—there are going to be challenges on the job, obstacles to overcome and hurtful situations to forgive. That's a given. It's called "living in a fallen world." In those times of testing and heartache, it would serve us well to be still and know that He is God. If we would recognize that God has given us a platform for a purpose, not just a position, and that positions are merely vehicles for impacting others, then we would be free to hold our positions with open hands. We would be free to align our heart with God's and embrace our competition as friends instead of foes.

TRULY, DEEPLY, MADLY

I'm not saying that we're never going to be hurt. Oh my gosh, I've cried buckets of tears and felt the deepest of pain. But what

I am saying is this: if we truly, deeply, madly know our purpose for work, we will be much more likely to recognize the heart of the matter when an on-the-job conflict arises. Remember, you don't just have a position; you have a purpose—to meaningfully impact the lives of those with whom you work.

You know, once I had a boss whom I had the most difficult time forming a relationship with. Conflict was the norm in our relationship. Bless her heart, we could not have been more different. I think I was her biggest challenge and I know for a fact, at times I was her greatest irritation. We were polar opposites. She hated religion—all religion; not just Christianity. She once told me that she had never seen anything good come out of religion. And there she was, stuck with me, a boisterous, no-holds-barred, all-in Christian.

It was the hardest working relationship I've ever known, and she probably felt the same way. I didn't want there to be tension—I really wanted a friendship, but I didn't know if she would ever let her guard down and let me be a friend. But I kept trying, because I genuinely believe that friendship is the key to producing "meaningful work, done in meaningful ways, with people you love." But man, it was like taking two steps forward and three steps back. I didn't know if we'd ever get to that place of friendship. I hoped we would and prayed we would, but I had my doubts.

I couldn't tell if we were making any progress or not. I lost count of all the times she made me cry. On the other hand, I'm sure I sent her up the ever-lovin' wall more times than I'd care to admit. Did I say it was hard? We were just so darn opposite.

So imagine my surprise, when one day I heard her say, "I know that Joan is a real Christian, because she always forgives me." I was blown away. I was so grateful for every day that we had ever shared, conflicts and all. All I had ever wanted was just to be her friend. Because, in my heart of hearts, I hoped that maybe . . . just maybe . . . she would feel the love of God.

TRUTH

Sometimes we get blindsided by a betrayal. Like a sucker punch to the gut, it catches us off guard and it hurts deeply. There are a lot of unfair moments in life that leave us reeling. Those moments seem to come out of nowhere, and they are *anything* but fun. In those moments, don't be hasty. Speak the truth to yourself. Remind yourself that you belong to God, and invisible though He may be, He is present with you in the moment. You are never alone.

Take a deep breath and hold your tongue. Step away if you have to, but wait to speak until you know what the Father would say regarding the matter at hand. I know how hard it can be when someone doesn't like you: it crushes the spirit and makes it hard to go on. But I promise you, if you will rein in your emotions with all the strength you can muster and take your hurt to God, He will give you the grace to see the matter through—regardless of the outcome.

My prayer is that you will never forget that your work is more than a paycheck—it is a partnership with God. You have been called to be an on-the-job difference-maker, so hold fast to Him when the winds of disappointment blow and adversity abounds. May you remember that He speaks peace in the midst of the storm and He has promised to take you safely to the other side. It has been a joy to share these stories with you, and I hope your heart has been encouraged. May you understand with an unshakable conviction that there is no dichotomy between the sacred and the secular—you work is holy, and it matters greatly to God.

EPILOGUE

"There is a time for everything,
and a season for every activity under the heavens."

Ecclesiastes 3:1 (NIV)

F rom 2006 to 2015, I was fortunate to lead a highly skilled team of talented stylists, estheticians, massage therapists, nail technicians, customer happiness representatives, housekeepers, valet parker and grounds crew. They were my dream team, and they brought me joy every single day! I am so grateful for my Rehoboth season in that salon, where my heart was mended and there was room enough for me to shine for God's glory. Those were sweet days! But nothing lasts forever.

I loved coaching, mentoring, and speaking. So, when a friend suggested I become a certified John Maxwell Leadership Coach, Mentor and Speaker, it was a no-brainer. In September 2014, I began the enrollment process. I am so thankful that I pursued the Maxwell certification, because my salon job was coming to end quicker than I could have imagined.

The year 2015 ushered in massive upheaval. In April, the salon closed its doors, and I was jobless. It was the year my family and I said *goodbye* to thirty years of beautiful friendships. And it was the year that we said *hello* to a brand new life a thousand miles away from the home we'd loved so well. Our future was as clear as mud. But the time had come to close that chapter, turn another page, and begin a new adventure.

In August, we pulled up stakes and moved to Tennessee, not knowing what the future would hold. (Truth be told, my husband and I had prayed for years that God would someday move us to Tennessee. While our feet may have been planted in Texas, our hearts were in Nashville with the family we loved.)

A couple weeks later, we were still living out of our suitcases, but it was time for me to head to Florida to receive my John Maxwell certification. I got my certification and headed back to Nashville, with just a little more hope in my soul that all would be well. I didn't know anyone in Nashville (except family). Every business relationship I had was back in Texas, so I had no one to vouch for me. I didn't know how I was gonna build a business. It was pretty obvious that if doors were going to open, it would have to be a God thing.

But that's what God does—He opens doors. Our challenges become something beautiful, a story that astounds the world and reminds them that our God is interested in every facet of our lives. In His grace, He has connected me with salon leaders to coach, mentor, and train on leadership styles that promote employee engagement and love in the workplace. Through my coaching business, I am helping leaders build better companies through the implementation of employee-focused programs that equip staff members to reach their full potential, achieve lifelong goals, and see their dreams come to fulfillment. My business is growing, and I am bowed low in adoration of God's goodness towards me.

NOTES

1. John Eldredge, *The Journey of Desire*, (Nashville: Thomas Nelson Publishers, 2000), 12.

2. Lisa Earle McLeod, *Leading with Noble Purpose*, (Hoboken, NJ: John Wiley & Sons, Inc., 2016), xi.

3. Lisa Earle McLeod *Leading with Noble Purpose*, (Hoboken, NJ: John Wiley & Sons, Inc., 2016), ix.

4. Joel Kessel, "What I Mean By Sharing Your Meaningful Work In A Meaningful Way," *Joel Kessel*, http://www.joelkessel.com/what-i-mean-by-sharing-your-meaningful-work-in-a-mea ningful-way

5. Sherman, Robert B., and Richard M. Sherman. *Mary Poppins*. DVD. Directed by Robert Stevenson. Walt Disney Studios, 1964.

6. Dr. Charles Stanley, "Life Principle 10: God Will Show You His Will," *In Touch*, July 10, 2014, https://www.intouch.org/read/life-principle-10-god-will-show-you-his-will

7. If you want to read more about calling, here is an excellent article to get your feet wet: Anne Graham Lotz, "How to Seek God's Guidance," *Decision*, February 2003, 38-39, http://www.annegrahamlotz.org/wp-content/uploads/2014/11/runway-lights1.pdf

8. Dr. Charles R. Ringma, Professor Emeritus at Regent College, Vancouver Canada.

9. Amy Adkins, "Majority of U.S. Employees Not Engaged Despite Gains in 2014," *Gallup*, January 28, 2015, http://www.gallup.com/

poll/181289/majority-employees-not-engaged-despite-gains-2014. aspx?

10. Alyson Shontell, "80% Hate Their Jobs—But Should You Choose A Passion Or A Paycheck?" Oct. 4, 2010, http://www.businessinsider. com/what-do-you-do-when-you-hate-your-job-2010-10

11. Dennis Bakke, "The Purpose of Secular Work," in *Our Souls at Work*, ed. Mark L Russel, (Boise, ID: Russel Media), 25

12. Eugene Peterson, *A Long Obedience in The Same Direction*, (Downers Grove, IL: Isity Press, 1980), 108.

13. Dennis Bakke, "On The Purpose of Secular Work," in *Our Souls at Work*, ed. Mark L Russel, (Boise, ID: Russel Media), 25

14. Dr. Charles R. Ringma, Professor Emeritus at Regent College, Vancouver Canada.

15. Os Guinness, *The Call*, (Nashville: Word Publishing, 1998), 20, 29, 31.

16. Timothy Keller with Katherine Leary Alsdorf, *Every Good Endeavor*, (New York: Riverhead Books, 2012), 25.

17. Os Guinness, *The Call*, (Nashville: Word Publishing, 1998), 28, 29.

18. Trevor Cairney, "Don't Waste Your Life at Work," *The Gospel Coalition Australia*, May 15, 2015, https://australia. thegospelcoalition.org/article/dont-waste-your-life-at-work (Quotes Justin Taylor)

19. Abraham Kuyper, *A Centennial Reader*, ed. James D. Bratt (Eerdmans, 1998), 488.

20. Matte, Greg. "More Than a Paycheck." Sermon, Houston's First Baptist Church, Houston, TX.

21. Trevor Cairney, "Don't Waste Your Life at Work," *The Gospel Coalition Australia*, May 15, 2015, https://australia. thegospelcoalition.org/article/dont-waste-your-life-at-work (Quotes Justin Taylor)

22. Timothy Keller with Katherine Leary Alsdorf, *Every Good Endeavor*, (New York: Riverhead Books, 2012), 54-55.

23. Eugene Peterson, *A Long Obedience in The Same Direction*, (Downers Grove, IL: Isity Press, 1980), 109.

24. William C. Placher, *Callings: 20 Centuries of Christian Wisdom on Vocation*, (Grand Rapids, MI: Wm. B. Eerdmans Publishing Co., 2005), Preface, XV.

25. William C. Placher, *Callings: 20 Centuries of Christian Wisdom on Vocation*, (Grand Rapids, MI: Wm. B. Eerdmans Publishing Co., 2005), 3.

26. William C. Placher, *Callings: 20 Centuries of Christian Wisdom on Vocation*, (Grand Rapids, MI: Wm. B. Eerdmans Publishing Co., 2005), 23-24.

27. William C. Placher, *Callings: 20 Centuries of Christian Wisdom on Vocation*, (Grand Rapids, MI: Wm. B. Eerdmans Publishing Co., 2005), 112.

28. William C. Placher, *Callings: 20 Centuries of Christian Wisdom on Vocation*, (Grand Rapids, MI: Wm. B. Eerdmans Publishing Co., 2005), 112.

29. William C. Placher, *Callings: 20 Centuries of Christian Wisdom on Vocation*, (Grand Rapids, MI: Wm. B. Eerdmans Publishing Co., 2005), 6-7.

30. Fr. Don Miller, OFM, "Saint Catherine of Siena," *Franciscan Media,* http://www.americancatholic.org/Features/Saints/saint.aspx?id=1368

31. Jimmy Akin, "8 Things to Know and Share About St. Catherine of Siena," *National Catholic Register*, April 27, 2013, http://www.ncregister.com/blog/jimmy-akin/8-things-to-know-and-share-about-st.-catherine-of-siena

32. Os Guinness, *The Call*, (Nashville: Word Publishing, 1998), 32.

33. Os Guinness, *The Call*, (Nashville: Word Publishing, 1998), 34.

34. Os Guinness, *The Call*, (Nashville: Word Publishing, 1998), 34, 35.

35. "Postmodernism," *Theopedia*, http://www.theopedia.com/postmodernism

36. Steve Cornell, "What Does Postmodernism Mean?" *Summit*, October 24, 2006, http://www.summit.org/resources/truth-and-consequences/what-does-postmodern-mean/

37. Timothy Keller with Katherine Leary Alsdorf, *Every Good Endeavor*, (New York: Riverhead Books, 2012), 225.

38. Timothy Keller with Katherine Leary Alsdorf, *Every Good Endeavor*, (New York: Riverhead Books, 2012), 227.

39. Russell, Mark L., and Dave Gibbons, *Our Souls At Work*, (Boise, ID: Russel Media), 52, 53.

40. Dennis Bakke, "The Most Fun Workplace in Human History," in *Our Souls at Work*, ed. Mark L Russel, (Boise, ID: Russel Media)

41. "Why Desmond Tutu Became an Anglican Priest," *StoriesForPreaching.com*, https://storiesforpreaching.com/why-desmond-tutu-became-an-anglican-priest/ (This is a well-known story, reported even by Tutu himself.)

42. Lisa Earle McLeod, *Leading with Noble Purpose*, (Hoboken, NJ: John Wiley & Sons, Inc., 2016), 10.

43. E.M. Bounds, *Power Through Prayer*, (Moody Publishers, Chicago, IL), 40.

44. This principle was originated by Dr. Nicolas Ellen, Professor of Biblical Counseling at the College of Biblical Studies. You can visit his site at http://mycounselingcorner.com

ABOUT THE AUTHOR

Joan Turley is an encourager with a capital E! She is all about developing and empowering people. While serving as the director of operations for a prestigious Houston day spa and salon, Joan sharpened her leadership skills, created strong and well-educated teams, and elevated her staff to the top of their game. She has served as a guest lecturer for the University of Houston's Spa Management program, and she is a certified John Maxwell speaker, mentor, and leadership coach. Joan is a bold advocate for reversing the alarming job dissatisfaction rate within most companies. She coaches, mentors, and consults with salons, businesses, and individuals on her signature leadership style: leading with love, and implementing programs that empower others to become the best versions of themselves (both personally and professionally). With a heart full of compassion and a deep-seated belief that people are worth every ounce of energy to develop their potential, Joan is a motivational keynote speaker who speaks on creating and sustaining positive change within the workplace, as well as a message of hope and encouragement for women-led retreats and conferences. She and her husband live in Nashville, TN, and are blessed with two children and one amazing grandchild.

For more information, email Joan at joan@joanlturley.com
or visit www.JoanLTurley.com

Raving Fans

EXTRAORDINARY COMMUNICATION

"Joan is a natural mentor, fantastic speaker, and she draws in whomever she's speaking to with memorable anecdotes, stories, and examples. Her deep experience in leadership and the spa industry allows her to share valuable knowledge and insight with a large variety of audiences."

Su Gibson,
Instructor of Hospitality Management at
University of South Carolina Beaufort

RELATIONSHIP BUILDER

"Joan Turley is a natural-born leader and coach. Although she has worked hard to gain the skills that set her apart, her authentic love for people shines through in all she does. Whether she's training someone individually or in the workplace, they are sure to feel the care and warmth radiating from her core. Joan lights up a room and makes you feel like the most important person there. I can't say enough about the positive impact she has had on me, personally, and in our business. She has helped us bridge the gap between owners and employees. She brings the peace and calm to any storm."

Heather McCollum,
Owner of Fruition Salon (Nashville, TN)

HEART-DRIVEN LEADERSHIP FOR CREATIVE INDIVIDUALS

"Our company is very focused on systems, and we consider it a major reason for our success. With that said, the real key to any business endeavor is leadership. Systems without heart-driven leadership will not inspire individuals to reach their full potential or to feel loyalty to the company. Joan's in-salon training has challenged us to embrace both love and accountability, and we are forever grateful for her lessons on salon leadership. Her teachings have made a difference in our business and in our hearts."

Jón Snetman,
Co-owner of Jon Alan Salons (Nashville, TN)

ALWAYS OVER-DELIVERS

"Joan Turley has been a Godsend in our lives and business. Her love is contagious! Ever-ready to provide value, she always, *always* over-delivers. In a short amount of time, she has taken our salon to remarkable heights. The wisdom Joan provides within these pages will take you to new levels as you put them into practice."

Dalia & Vanessa Franco,
Owners of Raw Mane Salon (Kerrville, TX)

REMARKABLE MENTOR

"Joan has been such a lasting influence in both my professional and personal life. As an encourager, she continuously told me I was a superstar and believed in me. What a tremendous mentor for an 18-year-old. She never made it seem like work, and her door was always open to anyone who needed to talk. Striving to instill her core values as a manager, I attempt to mimic her love, respect and Godly traits. The legacy continues!"

Sarah Ward,
Co-Owner & Stylist at D-Vine Salon & Spa (Houston, TX)

AUTHENTIC LEADERSHIP

"It has been a pleasure to work with Joan, a true professional, on the growth and changes at the salon where she served as Director of Operations. Her attention to detail, organizational skills, problem solving ideas and genuine caring for those who work for the organization are a model of leadership."

Lydia Baehr,
President of Lydia Baehr Public Relations

OUTSTANDING PROFESSIONALISM

"Joan is a force of nature, graciously handling clients in every direction with poise, efficiency, and professionalism. She remains steady amidst change, always maintaining a consistent and strong work ethic. I would want Joan on any team for her focus, loyalty, talent, humor, and dependability."

Helen Perry,
Corporate & Personal Image Consultant (Houston, TX)

CPSIA information can be obtained
at www.ICGtesting.com
Printed in the USA
LVOW10s1359280917
550377LV00001B/5/P